I0007140

SECOND EDITION

Lua
Quick Reference

Mitchell

Lua Quick Reference
by Mitchell

Contact the author at books@triplequasar.com.

Editor: Ana Balan
Technical Reviewer: Robert Gieseke
Cover Designer: Mitchell
Interior Designer: Mitchell
Indexer: Mitchell

Printing history:
July 2017: First Edition
May 2020: Second Edition

ISBN: 978-0-9912379-5-1

Preface to the Second Edition

This book is an updated version of *Lua Quick Reference* and covers many of the features, changes, and incompatibilities introduced in Lua 5.4. Among the new content contained in this edition:

- Local variable attributes, including const and to-be-closed variables.
- Defining to-be-closed variable behavior.
- Lua's new warning system.
- The improved random number generator.
- Changes to Lua's string and thread facilities.
- Compiling Lua programs.
- More details about user values in the Lua C API.
- Various Lua C API additions and changes, including incompatible changes to the threading API.

The book's code examples have also been updated to use Lua 5.4 where applicable.

Contents

Part II: The Lua C API

To Brandon Washington

The unbeatable boss

Introduction

Lua[1] is a small, fast, powerful, and embeddable scripting language. It is well-suited for use in video games, application scripting, embedded devices, and nearly anywhere else a scripting language is needed.

Weighing in at just 400KB in compiled size and comprising less than 15,000 lines of highly portable ISO (ANSI) C source code, Lua is a very small language that compiles unmodified on nearly any platform with a C compiler. Many independent benchmarks recognize Lua as one of the fastest scripting languages available. Not only is Lua small and fast, but it is also powerful. With dynamic typing, lexical scoping, first-class functions, collaborative multi-threading, automatic memory management, and an incredibly flexible data structure, Lua is a truly effective object-oriented language, functional language, and data-driven language.

In addition to its assets of size, speed, and power, Lua's primary strength is that it is an embedded language. Lua is implemented as a C library, so a host program can use Lua's C Application Programming Interface (C API) to initialize and interact with a Lua interpreter, define global variables, register C functions that Lua can call, call user-defined Lua functions, and execute arbitrary Lua code. (In fact, Lua's stand-alone interpreter is just a C application that makes use of the Lua library and its C API.) This tight coupling between Lua and its host allows each language to leverage its own strengths: C's raw speed and ability to interact with third-party software, and Lua's flexibility, rapid prototyping, and ease of use.

Lua Quick Reference is designed to help the software developer "get things done" when it comes to programming in and embedding Lua, whether it is Lua 5.4, 5.3, 5.2, or 5.1. This book can even be used with LuaJIT,[2] a Just-In-Time compiler for Lua based on Lua 5.1. *Lua Quick Reference*'s pragmatic approach assumes the developer has a basic understanding of programming concepts. While familiarity with Lua is helpful, it is not a requirement—this book is suitable for helping seasoned developers quickly get up to speed with the language.

---

1   *http://www.lua.org*
2   *http://luajit.org/luajit.html*

This quick reference is broken up into two parts: Part I covers the Lua language itself and Part II covers Lua's C API. Each part has a number of descriptive sections with conveniently grouped tasks that cover nearly every aspect of Lua and its C API, with differences between versions clearly marked. For the most part, the contents of each task are not listed in conceptual order. They are listed in procedural order, an order the developer would likely follow when programming in or embedding Lua.

While this book aims to be a complete reference, it does omit some of the lesser-known parts of Lua. For example, this reference does not cover Lua's debug interface, weak tables, or some of the finer details of how external modules are loaded. *Lua Quick Reference* serves as a complement to each Lua version's Reference Manual.

Finally, all code examples in this book are based on Lua 5.4, so adapting them for Lua 5.1, 5.2, and Lua 5.3 may be necessary.

Download

Lua is free software and is available in source format from its website: *http://www.lua.org/download.html*. Links to platform-specific binaries are also available from that page. Lua is highly extensible and can be configured by modifying its *lua conf.h* file prior to compiling the library. For example, on more restricted platforms and embedded devices, the flag "LUA_32BITS" can be defined in order to force Lua to use 32-bit integers and 32-bit floating point numbers.

Code Editors

Programming in Lua does not require an Integrated Development Environment (IDE). A simple text editor is sufficient. The author recommends Textadept,[3] a fast, minimalist, and remarkably extensible cross-platform text editor that has fantastic support for Lua. Not only is Textadept free and open-source, but it is also one of the few cross-platform editors that have both a graphical and terminal user interface, the latter being helpful for working on remote machines.

3   *https://orbitalquark.github.io/textadept*

Conventions

This book uses the following conventions.

Italic
> Used for filenames and for introducing new terms.

`Constant width`
> Used for environment variables, command line options, and Lua and C code, including functions, tables, and variables.

`Constant width`   **Right-aligned annotation**
> Used for Lua or C code that applies to a particular version of Lua, which the annotation specifies. If there is no annotation, that code applies to all versions.

`Constant width italic`
> Used for user-specified arguments, parameters, expressions, and statements.

`[ ]`
> Used for optional function arguments, optional parameters, and optional statements, except in code examples that index Lua tables or contain C arrays. Unless otherwise specified, optional arguments default to `nil`.

Terminology

This book uses the following terminology.

Host
> The (typically C) program that interacts with a Lua interpreter. The stand-alone Lua interpreter is an example of a host.

Block
> A group of statements executed in sequential order. Blocks include function bodies and control structure bodies.

C function
> A special kind of function written in C that Lua can interact with.

List

A special kind of table that has non-nil values assigned to an unbroken sequence of integer keys from 1 to *n*, where *n* is the number of elements in the list. Lists may still have non-integer keys, but those keys and their associated values are ignored in list operations.

Upvalue

A non-local, non-global variable that a function has access to. In Lua upvalues are lexically scoped variables defined outside of functions, and in C they are values explicitly associated with C functions.

The stack

The C stack of Lua values associated with the applicable Lua interpreter, C function, or thread.

Environment Variables

Lua is configured to utilize the following environment variables.

LUA_PATH	
LUA_PATH_5_2	**Lua 5.2**
LUA_PATH_5_3	**Lua 5.3**
LUA_PATH_5_4	**Lua 5.4**

The value used for `package.path`. If more than one of these environment variables are defined, priority is given to the versioned variable.

The substring ";;" represents the default path that Lua was configured and compiled with, which is platform-dependent.

LUA_CPATH	
LUA_CPATH_5_2	**Lua 5.2**
LUA_CPATH_5_3	**Lua 5.3**
LUA_CPATH_5_4	**Lua 5.4**

The value used for `package.cpath`. If more than one of these environment variables are defined, priority is given to the versioned variable.

The substring ";;" represents the default path that Lua was configured and compiled with, which is platform-dependent.

```
LUA_INIT
LUA_INIT_5_2                                          Lua 5.2
LUA_INIT_5_3                                          Lua 5.3
LUA_INIT_5_4                                          Lua 5.4
```
The Lua script or Lua code to be executed before executing the script passed to the stand-alone Lua interpreter (*lua*, *lua.exe*, or any of its versioned variants). Lua scripts to be executed are indicated in "@*filename*" format. If more than one of these environment variables are defined, priority is given to the versioned variable.

Command Line Options

The stand-alone Lua interpreter accepts the following command line options and processes them sequentially. In most cases, order matters, the exceptions being -i and -E.

NOTE

When the interactive Lua prompt is active, each statement entered into the prompt is in its own scope. This particularly affects local variables, which are not visible to successive statements outside of a function body block, control structure block, or bare do ... end block. The section "Variables and Scopes" on page 10 describes scopes.

Also, in Lua 5.1 and 5.2, prefixing an expression with '=' will print its result after evaluation. Lua 5.3 and 5.4 print results implicitly.

Pressing Ctrl+Z on Windows, Ctrl+D on Linux or Mac, or entering the statement "os.exit()" quits the prompt.

-e *statement*
    Executes string *statement* as Lua code.

-l *module_name*
    Loads the Lua module whose string name is *module_name*. The section "Modules" on page 42 describes modules and how Lua searches for them.

-i
    Enters the interactive Lua prompt after running the given Lua script (if any).

-v

Prints Lua's version information.

-E   **Lua 5.2, 5.3, 5.4**

Ignores the environment variables listed in the previous section.

-W   **Lua 5.4**

Print to standard error (stderr) any warnings emitted while running Lua code. The sections "Error Handling and Warnings" and "Error and Warning Handling" on pages 48 and 129, respectively, describe Lua's warning system.

--

Stops handling command line options.

script [*args*]

Executes Lua script *script* with *args* as the script's argument list (which is stored in the global variable **arg**). If no script is given, starts an interactive Lua prompt.

-

Stops handling command line options and uses standard input (stdin) as the Lua script to be executed.

The Lua Language

Fundamentals

Lua is a free-form language with whitespace being significant only between identifiers and keywords. Lua source code files typically have the extension "*.lua*".

Comments

Lua has both line comments and block comments. Line comments start with "--" and apply until the end of the line they occur on. Block comments start with "--[[" and end with "]]". Block comment delimiters can contain an optional, equal number of '=' characters between the brackets:

```
-- Line comment.
i = 1 -- another line comment

--[[Multi-line
block comment.]]
t = {1, 2, --[[in-line block comment]] 3}

--[=[ Block comment that contains "]]". ]=]
```

Identifiers and Reserved Words

Identifiers are names of variables, table fields, and labels[†]. They are case-sensitive, and can be any combination of ASCII letters, digits, and underscores, though they cannot start with a digit or be a reserved word. Table 1 lists Lua's reserved words.

Some examples of valid identifiers are "a", "_", "A_i", "a1", and "END". Some examples of invalid identifiers are "1a", "µ", "function", and "$amount".

NOTE

By convention, identifiers comprising an underscore followed by one or more upper-case letters (e.g. "_M" and "_VERSION") are reserved for use by Lua itself.

---

†   Except for Lua 5.1, which does not have labels.

Table 1. Reserved words

and	break	do	else	elseif
end	false	for	function	goto[a]
if	in	local	nil	not
or	repeat	return	then	true
until	while			

[a] Not in Lua 5.1.

Variables and Scopes

Lua has both global and local variables. Global variables do not need to be declared; they can simply be used. Local variables must be declared with the keyword "`local`" (unless they are function arguments or `for` loop iterator variables, in which case they are implicitly local). Local variable declarations do not have to specify an initial value.

CAUTION

Variables in Lua are global by default. Lua will never raise an error if an attempt is made to reference a global variable with no previously defined value. Instead, the result will always be the value `nil`. Example 10 on page 46 gives an example of how to catch these cases.

It is better practice to use local variables wherever possible. Not only does this avoid potential name clashes between different parts of a program, but also local variable access is faster than global variable access.

Local variables are *lexically scoped*, meaning they are available only from within their current *block* starting after their point of declaration, and within any sub-blocks. Blocks are entities such as function bodies, control structure body parts, and Lua files. Local variables of the same name declared in different scopes are completely independent of one another. The following example and its accompanying call-outs exhibit the availability of local variables in various scopes:

```
-- Scoping example.
x = 1 ❶
local function y(z) ❷
  if condition then
    local x = x ❸
    block
  else
    block
    local z = x ❹
    block
  end
end
```

❶   x is a global variable. It is available anywhere a local variable x is not in scope.

❷   y is a local function and z is an implicit local argument variable. y is available inside itself (including its sub-blocks) and after its complete definition. z is available only inside y and its sub-blocks.

❸   x is a local variable whose initial value is the one assigned to global variable x. (This statement is a common idiom in Lua.) Any reassignments to local x do not affect global x. Local x is available only in the subsequent block below it. Outside that block (including within the else block), x refers to global x.

❹   z is a local variable whose initial value is global x (not local x in the if block). z is available only in the subsequent block below it (and not in the block above). Outside the lower block, z refers to local argument z.

Local Variable Attributes

Lua 5.4 introduced the ability to append the attributes "const" and "close" to local variable declarations:

```
local PI_2 <const> = math.pi / 2
local f <close> = io.open(filename)
```

<const> prevents the variable from being assigned a new value after its initial value assignment. <close> closes the variable's value when the variable goes out of scope (e.g. via break, return, loop end, error, etc.). This *to-be-closed variable* is particularly useful for automatic resource management, as demonstrated by Example 6 on page 35. Any other attribute is considered a syntax error.

Types

Lua is a *dynamically typed* scripting language. Lua variables have no defined type, and can be assigned and reassigned any Lua value. Lua values are *first-class values*, meaning they can be assigned to variables, passed as function arguments, returned as results, and so on. The following example illustrates these concepts:

```lua
a = nil
a = true
a = 0
a = "string"
a = function(x, y) return x + y, x - y end
a = {1, 2, 3}
a = coroutine.create(function(x)
  coroutine.yield(x^2)
end) -- note the function that is an argument
a = io.open("filename")
```

Lua has eight basic value types: *nil*, *boolean*, *number*, *string*, *function*, *table*, *thread*, and *userdata*. Each of these types is described in the following sections.

Nil

The nil type has a single value: `nil`. It typically indicates the absence of a useful value. The default value for variables and table keys is `nil`. Assigning `nil` to a variable or table key effectively deletes it.

Booleans

Booleans have one of two values: `true` or `false`. Other than `false` and `nil`, any other value is considered to be true in a boolean sense, including the number zero, the empty string, and an empty table.

Numbers

Numbers comprise both integer numbers and floating point numbers, or *floats*. Floats are typically double-precision floating point numbers, though this is configurable when compiling Lua. This book uses the term "float" in place of whatever type of float Lua is configured to use, which is not necessarily C's single-precision float.

Numbers can be written in decimal, exponential, or hexadecimal[†] notation. Integer numbers include "`0`" and "`-10`". Decimal floats include "`-1.0`" and "`3.14`". Exponential floats include "`6.67e-11`" and "`3E8`". Hexadecimal numbers include "`0xFF`", "`0x1P+8`", and "`0X0.a`".

NOTE

Lua 5.3 and 5.4 represent numbers internally as either integers or floats and seamlessly convert between the two types as needed. The range of integers that can be represented exactly is `math.mininteger` (typically -2^{63}) to `math.maxinteger` (typically 2^{63}). Integers wrap on overflow or underflow. The function `math.type()` returns whether a given number is represented as an integer or float internally.

Lua 5.1 and 5.2 represent all numbers (including integers) internally as floats. As a result, the range of integers that can be represented exactly is typically -2^{53} to 2^{53} (for a double-precision float). Any integer outside that range loses precision.

Lua can perform arithmetic with numbers, which is described in the section "Arithmetic Operators" on page 17. Its other numeric capabilities are listed in the section "Numeric Facilities" on page 51.

Strings

Strings are immutable, arbitrary sequences of bytes. They can contain embedded zeros and have no specific encoding attached to them. Strings can be constructed using double quotes, single quotes, or brackets:

```
dq = "double-quoted string"
sq = 'single-quoted string'
ms = [[multi-line
string]]
```

[†]   Except for Lua 5.1, which cannot express hexadecimal floats.

Quoted strings can contain any of the escape sequences listed in Table 2.

Bracketed strings cannot contain escape sequences, but can span multiple lines without the need for an escape sequence. If a bracketed string immediately starts with a newline, that initial newline is ignored. Similarly to block comments, bracketed string delimiters can contain an optional, equal number of '=' characters between the brackets.

Table 2. Quoted string escape sequences

Sequence	Meaning	Sequence	Meaning
\a	Bell	\"	Double quote
\b	Backspace	\'	Single quote
\f	Form feed	\(newline)	Literal newline
\n	Newline	\z[a]	Ignore subsequent whitespace
\r	Carriage return	\ddd	Decimal byte
\t	Horizontal tab	\xhh[a]	Hexadecimal byte
\v	Vertical tab	\u{uuuu}[b]	Hexadecimal UTF-8 codepoint
\\	Literal '\'		

[a] Not in Lua 5.1.

[b] Not in Lua 5.1 or 5.2.

Lua can concatenate strings, and this operation is covered in the section "Other Operators" on page 21. Its facilities for creating strings, querying and transforming strings, and searching and replacing within strings are described in the section "String Facilities" on page 54.

Functions

Functions consist of both Lua functions and C functions. (Lua does not distinguish between the two.) As first-class values, functions are anonymous (they do not have names). The sections "Functions" on page 27 and "C Functions" on page 114 describe Lua and C functions, respectively.

Tables

Tables are Lua's primary data type and implement *associative arrays*. An associative array is a set of key-value pairs where keys can be any value except `nil` and NaN,[4] and values can be any value except `nil`. (Therefore, if a table key is assigned `nil`, that key will no longer exist in the table.) Tables can be constructed using brace characters:

```
empty = {}
list  = {1, 2, 3}
dict  = {["a"] = 1, ["b"] = 2, ["c"] = 3}
mix   = {[0] = 0, 1, 2, 3, a = 1, b = 2, c = 3}
```

When keys are omitted in a table constructor, they implicitly become the integer values 1, 2, ..., *n* for the *n* values given without keys. (This kind of table with successive integer keys is considered a *list* and its values are considered *elements*.) Otherwise, keys are enclosed between brackets and are explicitly assigned values. (Both keys and values can be the results of expressions.) As a shortcut, an identifier may be used for a key. In this case, that *field* becomes a string key (e.g. the assignment "`a = 1`" is equivalent to "`["a"] = 1`"). If the last (or only) expression in a table constructor is a function call, all of the values returned by the called function are added as trailing list elements.

NOTE

Lua's list indices start at 1, unlike C's array indices, which start at 0.

Tables are mutable and can be altered using the various operators, statements, and functions covered throughout this book. Lua always assigns, passes, and returns references to tables instead of copies of tables. Tables automatically grow in size as needed, and Lua handles all of the memory management associated with them.

Threads

Threads are separate, independent lines of execution. Instead

---

4   Not a Number is a special value for undefined numbers like `0/0`.

of true multi-threading (asynchronous threads), Lua supports collaborative threads, or *coroutines*. Coroutines work together by resuming one another and then yielding to one another (a coroutine cannot be interrupted from the outside). Despite the fact that they run independently from one another, coroutines share the same global environment, and only one can be active at a time. Lua's main thread is a coroutine. The sections "Thread Facilities" and "Threading in C" on pages 68 and 133, respectively, describe Lua threads in more detail.

Userdata

Userdata act in place of C data types that cannot be represented by any other Lua value. As userdata, those C types can be treated like any other Lua value. (For example, Lua's file input and output objects are userdata.) Userdata values cannot be modified by Lua itself. The section "Push a userdata" on page 98 describes userdata in more detail.

Perform Basic Value Operations

Lua provides the means to retrieve the type of an arbitrary value, obtain the string representation of a value, and convert a string value to a number value.

type(*value*)
> Returns the string type of value *value*. The returned string is either "nil", "boolean", "number", "string", "table", "function", "thread", or "userdata".

tostring(*value*)
> Returns the string representation of value *value*, invoking the metamethod __tostring() if it exists. The section "Metatables and Metamethods" on page 32 describes metamethods.

tonumber(*value*[, *base*])
> Returns string *value* converted to a number in base number *base*, or nil if the conversion fails. *base* must be an integer between 2 and 36, inclusive, and its default value is 10.

Expressions and Operators

Expressions are combinations of operators and operands, but they can also be stand-alone values and variables. Table 3 lists Lua's operators, their precedence, and their grouping. Those operators are broken down into categories and described in the following sections.

Table 3. Operator precedence

Priority	Operator	Grouping
1	() [] .	Left-to-right
2	^	Right-to-left
3	not # - ~[a] (unary)	Left-to-right
4	* / //[a] %	Left-to-right
5	+ -	Left-to-right
6	..	Right-to-left
7	<<[a] >>[a]	Left-to-right
8	&[a]	Left-to-right
9	~[a]	Left-to-right
10	|[a]	Left-to-right
11	== ~= < <= > >=	Left-to-right
12	and	Left-to-right
13	or	Left-to-right

[a] Not in Lua 5.1 or 5.2.

Grouping indicates how operators with equal precedence are grouped. For example, the expression "2*3*4" is equivalent to "(2*3)*4" (left-to-right grouping), and "2^3^4" is equivalent to "2^(3^4)" (right-to-left grouping).

Arithmetic Operators

Lua supports the usual arithmetic operators.

```
x + y
x - y
x * y
x / y
x // y                                        Lua 5.3, 5.4
x % y
x^y
```

Arithmetically adds, subtracts, multiplies, divides, integer divides, computes the remainder of floor division between, or exponentiates numeric or string operands x and y. (String operands are converted to numbers first.)

If either x or y is a table or userdata value with the applicable metamethod __add(), __sub(), __mul(), __div(), __idiv(), __mod(), or __pow(), that metamethod is called to perform the operation. The section "Arithmetic Metamethods" on page 33 describes arithmetic metamethods.

-x

Arithmetically negates numeric or string operand x. (String operands are converted to numbers first.)

If x is a table or userdata value with the metamethod __unm(), that metamethod is called to perform the operation. The section "Arithmetic Metamethods" on page 33 describes arithmetic metamethods.

Relational Operators

Lua allows values to be compared to one another.

```
a == b
a ~= b
```

Returns a boolean that indicates whether values a and b are equal or unequal.

If a and b are numbers, they are compared numerically, regardless of their internal representation (e.g. the integer 1 is equivalent to the float 1.0). If a and b are strings, they are compared byte-wise. Otherwise, a and b are compared by reference: they are equal only if they have the same originally created value. (For example, two separately created tables with the same contents are not considered equal.)

If either *a* or *b* is a table or userdata value with the metamethod __eq(), that metamethod is called to perform the operation. (The operator "~=" returns the negation of the result of __eq()). The section "Relational Metamethods" on page 33 describes relational metamethods.

a < *b*
a <= *b*
a > *b*
a >= *b*

Returns a boolean that indicates whether value *a* is less than value *b*, less than or equal to *b*, greater than *b*, or greater than or equal to *b*.

If *a* and *b* are numbers, they are compared numerically, regardless of their internal representation. If *a* and *b* are strings, they are compared according to the current locale.

If either *a* or *b* is a table or userdata value with the applicable metamethod __lt() or __le(), that metamethod is called to perform the operation. __lt() handles "less than" and "greater than" operations and __le() handles the other two. The section "Relational Metamethods" on page 33 describes relational metamethods.

If *a* could not be compared to *b*, an error is raised.

Logical Operators

Logical operators can be used in boolean expressions and in conditional expressions.

not *a*

Returns the negation of the result of converting value *a* to a boolean, where any value other than `false` and `nil` is considered `true`.

a and *b*

Returns value *a* if it is boolean false (i.e. `false` or `nil`), or value *b* otherwise. (The boolean result of the expression is true if both operands are boolean true.) If *a* is to be returned, the conditional short-circuits, and *b* is not evaluated.

a or *b*

Returns value *a* if it is boolean true (i.e. not `false` or `nil`), or value *b* otherwise. (The boolean result of the expression is true if either operand is boolean true.) If *a* is to be returned, the conditional short-circuits, and *b* is not evaluated.

TIP

The expression "a and b or c" is equivalent to the C ternary operator expression "a ? b : c" as long as b is not boolean false.

Bitwise Operators

Lua 5.3 introduced bitwise operators for 64-bit integers[5] as a substitute for many of Lua 5.2's bitwise functions, which were provided by the module `bit32` and supported only 32-bit integers. Lua 5.1 does not have any bitwise facilities for integers.

x & *y*	**Lua 5.3, 5.4**
bit32.band(*x*, *y*)	**Lua 5.2**
x | *y*	**Lua 5.3, 5.4**
bit32.bor (*x*, *y*)	**Lua 5.2**
x ~ *y*	**Lua 5.3, 5.4**
bit32.bxor(*x*, *y*)	**Lua 5.2**

Performs bitwise AND, OR, or XOR on integer operands *x* and *y*. For each bit in *x* and *y*, bitwise AND returns 1 if both bits are 1, bitwise OR returns 1 if either bit is 1, and bitwise XOR returns 1 if either bit is 1, but not both.

If either *x* or *y* is a table or userdata value with the applicable metamethod __band(), __bor(), or __bxor(), that metamethod is called to perform the operation. The section "Bitwise Metamethods" on page 34 describes bitwise metamethods. Lua 5.2 does not have these metamethods.

---

5   64-bit integers can be used on 32-bit operating systems, provided the C data type `long long` is available. This is the case on many modern systems. More restricted platforms and embedded devices that support only up to 32-bit numbers can compile Lua with the "LUA_32BITS" flag defined in order to force Lua to use 32-bit integers.

~*x*   **Lua 5.3, 5.4**
bit32.bnot(*x*)   **Lua 5.2**
> Performs bitwise NOT on integer operand *x*. Bitwise
> NOT flips each bit in *x*.

> If *x* is a table or userdata value with the metamethod
> __bnot(), that metamethod is called to perform the oper-
> ation. The section "Bitwise Metamethods" on page 34 de-
> scribes bitwise metamethods. Lua 5.2 does not have this
> metamethod.

x << *y*   **Lua 5.3, 5.4**
bit32.lshift(*x*, *y*)   **Lua 5.2**
x >> *y*   **Lua 5.3, 5.4**
bit32.rshift(*x*, *y*)   **Lua 5.2**
> Shifts the bits in integer *x* by *y* bits to the left or right,
> and fills vacant bits with zeros.

> If either *x* or *y* is a table or userdata value with the appli-
> cable metamethod __shl() or __shr(), that metamethod
> is called to perform the operation. The section "Bitwise
> Metamethods" on page 34 describes bitwise metameth-
> ods. Lua 5.2 does not have these metamethods.

Other Operators

Lua has other operators for function calls, table indexing,
string concatenation, and value length.

f([*expr1, expr2, …, exprN*])
f{…}
f"*string*" or *f*'*string*' or *f*[[*string*]]
> Calls function *f* with an argument list, a single con-
> structed table argument, or a single string argument. The
> values in an argument list are the respective values that
> result from the evaluation of expressions *expr1*, *expr2*,
> …, *exprN*. If *exprN* is a function call that returns multiple
> values, all returned values are used in the argument list.
> (In any prior function call expression, only the first re-
> turned value is used.)

> Unless the function call is enclosed within parentheses,
> all of the values returned by *f* become the values re-
> turned by the function call. Otherwise, only the first
> value returned is used.

If *f* is a table or userdata value with the metamethod __call(), that metamethod is called to perform the operation. The section "Other Operator and Statement Metamethods" on page 35 covers this metamethod in its generic form.

t[*key*]
t.*name*

Retrieves the value in table *t* associated with key *key* or string *"name"*. *name* must be a valid identifier. *key* may also be an expression whose resulting value will be used as the lookup key.

If either *t* is a table value that does not contain *key* or *"name"*, or *t* is a userdata value, and *t* has the metafield __index or metamethod __index(), then that entity is used to perform the operation. The section "Other Operator and Statement Metamethods" on page 35 covers this metafield and metamethod.

CAUTION

Lua will never raise an error if an attempt is made to reference a table key with no assigned value (regardless of whether or not it had one previously). Instead, the result will always be nil. Example 10 on page 46 gives an example of how to catch these cases (though after substituting _G in the example with *t*).

---

a .. *b*

Returns strings or numbers *a* and *b* concatenated together into a new string. (Number operands are converted to strings first.)

If either *a* or *b* is a table or userdata value with the metamethod __concat(), that metamethod is called to perform the operation. The section "Other Operator and Statement Metamethods" on page 35 covers this metamethod in its generic form.

#*v*

Returns the length of value *v*. If *v* is a string, returns the number of bytes in *v*. If *v* is a list, returns the number of elements in it (ignoring any values assigned to non-integer keys in *v*).

Local variable declarations do not have to specify initial values. They are `nil` by default.

If *exprN* is a function call that returns multiple values, all returned values are used in the list of values to be assigned. (In any prior function call expression, only the first returned value is used.) If the number of values is less than the number of variables, the remaining variables each have the value `nil`. If the number of values is greater than the number of variables, the extra values are ignored.

Lua 5.4 allows attributes in a list of local variable declarations, though only one `<close>` attribute may exist.

TIP

The values of two variables a and b can be swapped using the statement "a, b = b, a".

Table key assignment

Values can be assigned to keys in tables similarly to how values can be retrieved from table keys.

```
t[key] = expr
t.name = expr
```
Evaluates expression *expr* and assigns the resulting value to key *key* or string *"name"* in table *t*. *name* must be a valid identifier. *key* may also be an expression whose resulting value is used as the lookup key.

If either *t* is a table value that does not contain *key* or *"name"*, or *t* is a userdata value, and *t* has the metafield __newindex or metamethod __newindex(), then that entity is used to perform the assignment. The section "Other Operator and Statement Metamethods" on page 35 covers this metafield and metamethod.

Control Structures

Lua has four different control structures: `if`, `for`, `while`, and `repeat`. It also provides the means to immediately jump out of the latter three loop structures. Example 1 demonstrates a

---

couple of these control structures while implementing a global function that computes a list of prime numbers using the Sieve of Eratosthenes method.

Example 1. Sieve of Eratosthenes

```
function sieve(n)
  -- Construct initial {2..n} table.
  local is_prime = {}
  for i = 2, n do
    is_prime[i] = true
  end

  -- Strike out all existing multiples of primes.
  for i = 2, math.sqrt(n) do
    if is_prime[i] then
      for j = i^2, n, i do
        is_prime[j] = false
      end
    end
  end

  -- Construct the final primes list.
  local primes = {}
  for i = 2, n do
    if is_prime[i] then
      primes[#primes + 1] = i
    end
  end
  return primes
end
```

```
if expr1 then block1
[elseif expr2 then block2 … elseif exprN then blockN]
[else blockE]
end
```

Evaluates expression *expr1* and, if the resulting value is boolean true (i.e. not false or nil), executes the statements in block *block1*. Otherwise, evaluates expression *expr2* and, if that resulting value is boolean true, executes the statements in block *block2*. Continues this process up through expression *exprN*. If no expression evaluation resulted in true, executes the statements in block *blockE*.

```
for variable = expr1, expr2[, expr3] do block end
```
Evaluates expressions *expr1*, *expr2*, and *expr3* and then

varies the value of the local variable named *variable* between the resultant values of *expr1* and *expr2* and, for each iteration, executes the statements in block *block* before incrementing *variable* by the resultant value of *expr3*. The value of *expr3* can be negative, and its default value is 1.

block must not alter the value of *variable*.

for *var1*, *var2*, …, *varN* in *iterator* do *block* end
Iterates over all sets of values produced by iterator *iterator* and, for each iteration, assigns each value in a set to the local variables named *var1*, *var2*, …, *varN*, respectively, and executes the statements in block *block*.

block must not alter the values of *var1*, *var2*, …, *varN*.

An iterator is a set of three values: function *f*, initial state *i*, and loop variable *v*. Lua 5.4 has an optional fourth value: to-be-closed *c*. For each iteration, *f(i, v)* is evaluated and the results are assigned to *var1*, *var2*, …, *varN*. If *var1* is nil, iteration ceases and *c* is closed (the section "Closing Metamethod" on page 35 describes how to define closing behavior). Otherwise, *var1* becomes *v* for the next iteration.

The Lua functions pairs(), string.gmatch(), io.lines(), etc. all return iterators.

while *expr* do *block* end
Repeatedly evaluates expression *expr* and, as long as the resulting value is boolean true (i.e. not false or nil), executes the statements in block *block*.

repeat *block* until *expr*
Repeatedly executes the statements in block *block* and, after each iteration, evaluates expression *expr* and verifies its resulting value is boolean true (i.e. not false or nil) before continuing with the next iteration.

Any local variables declared in *block* are available in *expr*.

break
Immediately jumps out of the current for, while, or repeat loop, and jumps to the statement after the end of the loop.

Labels and Goto

Lua 5.2 introduced labels and the keyword "goto". Contrary to popular belief, goto is not a poor design decision, but quite acceptable in certain situations, especially when emulating the "continue", "redo", and multi-level "break" statements some programming languages have that Lua does not. Example 2 demonstrates a proper use of goto as a substitute for the lack of "continue" in loops.

Example 2. Emulating "continue" with goto

```
local function open_files(filenames)
  for i = 1, #filenames do
    local text = ""
    local f = io.open(filenames[i])
    if f then
      text = f:read("a")
      if not text then goto continue end -- cannot read
      f:close()
    end
    --[[ process text... ]]
    ::continue::
  end
end
```

::*label*::   Lua 5.2, 5.3, 5.4

Defines a label named *label* in the current scope. *label* must be a valid identifier and, in Lua 5.4, unique to its scope. This label is visible from anywhere inside its scope (not just from its point of definition).

goto *label*   Lua 5.2, 5.3, 5.4

Jumps to the statement after the visible label named *label* as long as that label is not inside a function other than the current one (if any), outside the current function (if any), or in the middle of a block with a local variable already defined in the scope of that block.

Functions

A Lua function is little more than a block of statements assigned to a variable or table key. Functions can accept one or more argument values and can also return one or more values. (Example 1 on page 25 defines a global function that returns a single list of prime numbers up to an argument n.) Due to the nature of lexical scoping, functions have access to any local variables defined outside their bodies, as long as those variables are in scope. These non-local (in a sense) but non-global variables are referred to as *upvalues*, and are extremely useful. Example 3 utilizes upvalues in order to compute the numeric antiderivative (integral) for a given mathematical function and optional epsilon value.

NOTE

Functions are limited to defining 200 local variables (including arguments). This limit does not include upvalues.

Example 3. Numeric antiderivative (integral) function

```lua
local function F(f, dx)
  dx = dx or 1e-4
  -- Trapezoidal numeric integration function that uses
  -- upvalues 'f' and 'dx'.
  return function(b)
    local sum, a = 0, 0
    for x = a, b, dx do
      sum = sum + (f(x) + f(x + dx)) / 2 * dx
    end
    return sum
  end
end

-- x² = ∫ 2x dx
local x2 = F(function(x) return 2 * x end)
-- x2(0), x2(1), x2(2), x2(3) gives approx. 0, 1, 4, 9
```

TIP

The statement "a = a or b" is an idiom for assigning a default value b to function argument a, provided a is boolean false (i.e. false or nil).

```
function name        ([arg1, arg2, …, argN]) block end
name = function      ([arg1, arg2, …, argN]) block end
local function name  ([arg1, arg2, …, argN]) block end
local name = function([arg1, arg2, …, argN]) block end
```

Defines a function (or local function) that accepts arguments, and assigns that function to the variable named *name*.[6] When the function is called, it assigns any argument values given to the respective local variables named *arg1*, *arg2*, …, *argN*, and then executes the statements in block *block*. If the number of argument values is less than the number of variables, the remaining variables each have the value `nil`. If the number of argument values is greater than the number of variables, the extra values are ignored.

name may also be a table key (e.g. "*t.name*", "*t1.t2.name*", etc.). In that case, the keyword "`local`" cannot be used.

TIP

Functions can have "named arguments" if they accept only one table value and are called in the following manner: "*name{arg1=expr1, arg2=expr2, …, argN=exprN}*". This can be useful if a function has many optional arguments.

`return` [*expr1, expr2, …, exprN*]
Immediately jumps out of the current function and returns the resulting values of expressions *expr1, expr2, …, exprN* as the results of the function call. If *exprN* is a function call that returns multiple values, all of those returned values are included in the current function's returned results. (In any prior function call expression, only the first returned value is used.)

If only one expression is given, if that expression is a function call, and if there are no to-be-closed variables in scope, then Lua reuses the current call stack frame for the resulting *tail call*. As a result, it is not possible to overflow the call stack with tail calls (which is useful for recursive functions).

This statement can also appear at the end of a file. Lua modules, which are described in the section "Create a Lua Module" on page 45, make use of this, as does the function `dofile()`.

---

6   *name* is just a variable name, not the function's name. In Lua, functions are first-class values, which are inherently anonymous.

Functions with Variable Arguments

Lua functions can accept and work with a variable number of argument values and return a variable number of values. Example 4 shows a function that accepts a variable number of arguments and passes some of them to another function.

Example 4. Function that accepts variable arguments

```
function handle_event(event_name, ...)
  local f = event_handlers[event_name]
  if f then
    -- Forward all event parameters to the event
    -- handler function.
    return f(...)
  end
end
```

```
function name        ([arg1, arg2, …, argN, ]...) block end
name = function       ([arg1, arg2, …, argN, ]...) block end
local function name   ([arg1, arg2, …, argN, ]...) block end
local name = function([arg1, arg2, …, argN, ]...) block end
```

Defines a function (or local function) that accepts a variable number of arguments, and assigns that function to the variable named *name*. When the function is called, it assigns the first *N* argument values given to the respective local variables named *arg1*, *arg2*, …, *argN* and stores the remaining values in the expression "...". The function then executes the statements in block *block*. If the number of argument values is less than the number of variables, the remaining variables each have the value nil and "..." will be empty.

Any statements in *block* can use the expression "..." in place of the extra argument values the function was given. For example, "..." can be used in variable assignment statements, function calls, table constructors, and `return` statements.

name may also be a table key (e.g. "*t.name*", "*t1.t2.name*", etc.). In this case, the keyword "`local`" cannot be used.

NOTE

The expression "`...`" represents all of its values only when it occurs at the end of an expression list. Anywhere else it only represents its first value. For example, given a function *f*, the expression "*f*(x, `...`)" calls *f* with at least two arguments, while the expression "*f*(`...`, x)" calls *f* with exactly two arguments, regardless of how many values "`...`" represents.

`select("#", ...)`
`select(index, ...)`

> Returns the number of extra argument values given, or all of the extra argument values given after extra argument number *index*. In Lua 5.2, 5.3, and 5.4, if *index* is negative, counts from the end of the argument list.

`{...}`
`table.pack(...)`   **Lua 5.2, 5.3, 5.4**

> Returns a new list whose elements are the extra argument values given. The table returned by `table.pack()` also contains a field `"n"` that indicates the number of extra arguments. This is useful in the event that any of those values are `nil`, since lists cannot contain `nil` values.

`return [expr1, expr2, …, exprN,]...`

> Immediately jumps out of the current function and returns as the results of the function call the resulting values of expressions *expr1*, *expr2*, …, *exprN* along with any extra argument values given.

NOTE

The maximum number of return values is around 8,000 in Lua 5.1 and around 15,000 in Lua 5.2, 5.3, and 5.4. This arbitrary limit is related to Lua's maximum stack size and is configurable when compiling Lua. The section "The Stack" on page 90 describes Lua's stack.

Metatables and Metamethods

Lua's operators are not limited to specific types of values, nor are they limited to a specific operation. By using *metatables* and *metamethods*, operators can be *overloaded*, or have their operations changed, depending on the operands given. This concept also applies to some of Lua's built-in functions such as `tostring()`.

A metatable is a special kind of table with specific keys assigned to user-defined functions called metamethods. When a value is assigned a metatable, operators using that value as an operand can behave differently. Example 5 demonstrates how to overload the concatenation operator for one list in order to concatenate that list with another one. The following sections cover metatable assignment as well as the metamethods that affect Lua's operators and built-in functions.

NOTE

For the sake of brevity, metamethods are listed in "`func tion name() … end`" form. The "`name = function() … end`" form is also valid.

Example 5. Overload concatenation for a list

```lua
local t1, t2 = {1, 2, 3}, {4, 5, 6}
local mt = {}
function mt.__concat(a, b)
  local t = {}
  -- Add all elements of a to t.
  for i = 1, #a do t[#t + 1] = a[i] end
  -- Add all elements of b to t.
  for i = 1, #b do t[#t + 1] = b[i] end
  return t
end
setmetatable(t1, mt)
local t3 = t1 .. t2 -- results in {1, 2, 3, 4, 5, 6}
```

Assign and Retrieve Metatables

Lua allows any table or userdata value to have its own metatable. (Groups of tables and userdata can also share the same metatable.)

```
setmetatable(v, metatable)
```
Assigns metatable *metatable* to be the metatable of table or userdata *v*, and returns *v*. If *metatable* is `nil`, removes the metatable assigned to *v*. If *v* has a metatable and that metatable has the metafield __metatable, raises an error.

```
getmetatable(v)
```
Returns the metatable of table or userdata *v*, or `nil` if *v* has no metatable. If *v* has a metatable and that metatable has the metafield __metatable, returns that value instead.

Arithmetic Metamethods

Lua's arithmetic operators can be overloaded with arithmetic metamethods. These metamethods are invoked only if one of the operands is a table or userdata value with the applicable metamethod. The first value returned by the metamethod becomes the resulting value of the arithmetic operation.

```
function metatable.__add (x, y) block end
function metatable.__sub (x, y) block end
function metatable.__mul (x, y) block end
function metatable.__div (x, y) block end
function metatable.__idiv(x, y) block end          Lua 5.3, 5.4
function metatable.__mod (x, y) block end
function metatable.__pow (x, y) block end
```
Overloads the addition (+), subtraction (-), multiplication (*), division (/), integer division (//), modulo (%), and exponentiation (∧) operators for values whose metatables are table *metatable*. Local variables *x* and *y* refer to the operator's operands. If the value of *x* has the appropriate metamethod, that metamethod is used. Otherwise, the metamethod of the value of *y* is used.

```
function metatable.__unm(x) block end
```
Overloads the arithmetic negation operator (-) for values whose metatables are table *metatable*. Local variable *x* refers to the operator's operand.

Relational Metamethods

Lua's relational operators can be overloaded with relational metamethods. Typically, these metamethods are invoked only if one of the operands is a table or userdata value with the applicable metamethod. The first value returned by the meta-method is converted to a boolean, and that boolean becomes the resulting value of the relational operation.

```
function metatable.__eq(a, b) block end
function metatable.__lt(a, b) block end
function metatable.__le(a, b) block end
```
Overloads the equality (==) and inequality (~=), less than (<) and greater than (>), and less than or equal to (<=) and greater than or equal to (>=) operators for values whose metatables are table *metatable*. Local variables *a* and *b* refer to the operator's operands. If the value of *a* has the appropriate metamethod, that metamethod is used. Otherwise, the metamethod of the value of *b* is used.

__eq() is invoked only when *a* and *b* are of the same type. Only __lt() and __le() are needed for relational inequalities, since the expression "*a* > *b*" is translated to "*b* < *a*" and the expression "*a* >= *b*" is translated to "*b* <= *a*". Furthermore, in Lua 5.1, 5.2, and 5.3, the metamethod __le() may be omitted as long as __lt() exists, since the expression "*a* <= *b*" would be translated to "not (*b* < *a*)".

Bitwise Metamethods

The bitwise operators introduced in Lua 5.3 can be overloaded with bitwise metamethods. These metamethods are invoked only if one of the operator's operands is a table or userdata value with the applicable metamethod. The first value returned by the metamethod becomes the resulting value of the bitwise operation.

```
function metatable.__band(x, y) block end          Lua 5.3, 5.4
function metatable.__bor (x, y) block end          Lua 5.3, 5.4
function metatable.__bxor(x, y) block end          Lua 5.3, 5.4
```
Overloads the bitwise AND (&), OR (|), and XOR (~) operators for values whose metatables are table *meta table*. Local variables *x* and *y* refer to the operator's operands. If the value of *x* has the appropriate metamethod, that metamethod is used. Otherwise, the metamethod of the value of *y* is used.

function *metatable.*__bnot(*x*) *block* end   **Lua 5.3, 5.4**
> Overloads the bitwise NOT operator (~) for values whose metatables are table *metatable*. Local variable *x* refers to the operator's operand.

function *metatable.*__shl(*x, y*) *block* end   **Lua 5.3, 5.4**
function *metatable.*__shr(*x, y*) *block* end   **Lua 5.3, 5.4**
> Overloads the bitwise shift left (<<) and shift right (>>) operators for values whose metatables are table *meta table*. Local variables *x* and *y* refer to the operator's operands. If the value of *x* has the appropriate metamethod, that metamethod is used. Otherwise, the metamethod of the value of *y* is used.

Closing Metamethod

Lua 5.4's handling of local variables going out of scope can be overloaded with the attribute <close> and a closing metamethod. This enables easy resource cleanup, particularly if unexpected errors occur. Example 6 shows this with a Lua file handle, which defines its own __close() metamethod.

Example 6. Processing a file

```
local filenames = { --[[ list of filenames... ]] }
for i = 1, #filenames do
  local f <close> = io.open(filenames[i])
  if f then
    --[[ process file... ]]
  end
end
```

function *metatable.*__close(*v*) *block* end   **Lua 5.4**
> Overloads the behavior of values whose metatables are table *metatable* when they go out of scope (e.g. via break, return, loop end, error, etc.). Local variable *v* refers to the value of a to-be-closed variable.

Other Operator and Statement Metamethods

Some of Lua's other various operators and statements can be overloaded with the appropriate metamethods. These metamethods are invoked only if the operator's operand or one of its operands is a table or userdata value with the applicable metamethod. The first value returned by the metamethod becomes the resulting value of the operation, except for the function call operator, which returns all values returned by the metamethod. Example 7 illustrates how to create a read-only table.

Example 7. Create a read-only table

```
local t = { --[[ read-only table contents... ]] }
t = setmetatable({}, {
  __index = t,
  __newindex = function() error("read-only table") end
})
```

function *metatable*.__call(*v*[, *arg1*, *arg2*, …, *argN*])
function *metatable*.__call(*v*[, ...]) *block* end

> Overloads the function call operator for values whose metatables are table *metatable*. Local variable *v* refers to the value being called and local variables *arg1*, *arg2*, …, *argN* (as well as the expression "...") refer to the argument values being passed to the call.

function *metatable*.__index   (*t*, *key*)   *block* end
function *metatable*.__newindex(*t*, *key*, *value*) *block* end
metatable.__index   = *proxy*
metatable.__newindex = *proxy*

> Overloads the table index operators ([] and .) and table assignment statement for values whose metatables are table *metatable*. Local variable *t* refers to the value being indexed, local variable *key* refers to the key used in the indexing, and local variable *value* refers to the value to be assigned to *key*. (Lua does not actually perform the assignment, however.) Table *proxy* is the table indexed or assigned to in place of *t*, and may have its own indexing or assignment metamethods.

> These metamethods are invoked only if either *t* is not a table or *key* does not exist in table *t*.

function *metatable*.__concat(*a*, *b*) *block* end

> Overloads the string concatenation operator (..) for values whose metatables are table *metatable*. Local variables *a* and *b* refer to the operator's operands. If the value of *a* has the appropriate metamethod, that metamethod is used. Otherwise, the metamethod of the value of *b* is

used.

```
function metatable.__len(v) block end
```
Overloads the value length operator (#) for values whose metatables are table *metatable*. Local variable *v* refers to the operator's operand.

In Lua 5.1, table values cannot overload the length operator. Only userdata values can.

Function Metamethods

Some of Lua's built-in functions can be overloaded with the appropriate metamethods. These metamethods are invoked only if the argument value is a table or userdata value with the applicable metamethod.

```
function metatable.__pairs (t) block end
function metatable.__ipairs(t) block end                    Lua 5.2
```
Overloads the functions pairs() and ipairs() for argument values whose metatables are table *metatable*. Local variable *t* refers to the argument value passed. Only the first three values returned by the metamethod become the resulting values of the function call. Those values constitute an iterator. The section "Control Structures" on page 24 mentions iterators.

NOTE

In Lua 5.3 and 5.4, ipairs() respects the metafield __index and metamethod __index() when producing index-element pairs, so there is no longer a need for __ipairs().

```
function metatable.__tostring(v) block end
```
Overloads the function tostring() for argument values whose metatables are table *metatable*. Local variable *v* refers to the argument value passed.

```
metatable.__metatable = value
```
Overloads the functions getmetatable() and setmetatable() for argument values whose metatables are table *metatable*. getmetatable() will return value *value* and setmetatable() will raise an error.

Bypass Metamethods

Sometimes it is desirable (or even necessary) to bypass metamethods in order to work with values directly. For instance, Example 10 on page 46 makes it impossible to intentionally create a global variable using a simple assignment statement. For cases like these, Lua provides a set of functions that bypass metamethods.

`rawequal(value1, value2)`
Returns whether or not values *value1* and *value2* are equal, bypassing all metamethods.

`rawget(t, key)`
Returns the actual value associated with key *key* in table *t*, bypassing all metamethods.

`rawset(t, key, value)`
Assigns value *value* to be the actual value of key *key* in table *t*, bypassing all metamethods.

`rawlen(t)`   **Lua 5.2, 5.3, 5.4**
`#t`   **Lua 5.1**
Returns the actual length of list *t*, bypassing all metamethods.

Object-Oriented Programming

Lua supports object-oriented programming, though not in the traditional sense of supplying the means to create classes, methods, and objects. Instead, Lua can emulate an object-oriented system by using a blend of tables, metatables, and some special syntax. While there are many different approaches for emulating such a system, the subsequent sections describe a typical approach.

Define a Class

Example 8 demonstrates a common method for defining a class, and is followed by more details on that approach.

Example 8. A sample class for 2-D vector objects

```lua
-- Create the vector class object.
local vector = {}
vector.__index = vector

-- Create a new vector with the given components.
function vector.new(x, y)
  local v = {x = x, y = y}
  return setmetatable(v, vector)
end

-- Overload length operator to compute magnitude.
function vector.__len(v)
  return math.sqrt(v.x^2 + v.y^2)
end

-- Overload addition operator to add two vectors.
function vector.__add(v1, v2)
  assert(getmetatable(v1) == getmetatable(v2),
         "vectors expected")
  return vector.new(v1.x + v2.x, v1.y + v2.y)
end

-- Overload subtraction operator to subtract vectors.
function vector.__sub(v1, v2)
  assert(getmetatable(v1) == getmetatable(v2),
         "vectors expected")
  return vector.new(v1.x - v2.x, v1.y - v2.y)
end

-- Overload multiplication operator to compute vector
-- dot product or scale a vector.
function vector.__mul(v1, v2)
  if getmetatable(v1) == getmetatable(v2) then
    return v1.x * v2.x + v1.y * v2.y
  elseif tonumber(v1) or tonumber(v2) then
    local scalar = tonumber(v1) or v2
    local v = not tonumber(v1) and v1 or v2
    return vector.new(scalar * v.x, scalar * v.y)
  else
    error("vectors or scalar and vector expected")
  end
end

-- Normalize a vector in-place.
function vector:normalize()
  local magnitude = #self
```

```
      self.x = self.x / magnitude
      self.y = self.y / magnitude
    end

    -- Overload exponentiation operator to compute angle
    -- between vectors.
    function vector.__pow(v1, v2)
      assert(getmetatable(v1) == getmetatable(v2),
             "vectors expected")
      return math.acos(v1 * v2 / (#v1 * #v2))
    end

    -- Return a vector's direction angle from x-axis.
    function vector:angle()
      return self ^ vector.new(1, 0)
    end

    -- Return a vector's string representation.
    function vector:__tostring()
      return string.format("<%.3f, %.3f>", self.x, self.y)
    end

local class = {}
local class = setmetatable({}, superclass)
```

Creates a new table that represents a class whose name is *class* and optionally inherits methods and members from another previously defined class named *superclass*.

```
class.__index = class
```

Defines the metafield __index of the class named *class* such that any instance object of *class* (whose metatable will be assigned *class*) can access the methods and members of *class*.

```
function class.new([…])
  local instance = {}
  [block]
  return setmetatable(instance, class)
end
```

Defines a constructor function that creates and returns a new instance object of the class named *class*. Block *block* may populate that instance object with instance-specific members (fields) or perform any other instance-related actions. The returned object has a metatable that refers back to *class* in order to access the methods and members of *class* (and any superclasses).

```
function class.method(self[, …]) block end
function class:method([…])        block end
```
Defines the instance method named *method* for the class named *class*. *method* has a local variable named self that refers to a class instance object returned by *class*.new(). (Lua implicitly defines self when the character ':' is used instead of '.' when defining a method.)

Methods can be metamethods in order to overload Lua's operators when instance objects of *class* are used as the operator's operands.

If *class* has a superclass, and that superclass also has an instance method named *method*, the method being defined overrides the superclass method.

Multiple inheritance

Defining a class with multiple inheritance is similar to defining a class with single inheritance, except instead of utilizing the metafield __index, the metamethod __index() is used.

```
local class = setmetatable({}, {__index = function(_, k)
  for _, superclass in ipairs{super1, super2, …, superN}
    local v = superclass[k]
    if v then return v end
  end
end
```
Creates a new table that represents a class whose name is *class* and inherits methods and members from other previously defined classes named *super1*, *super2*, …, *su perN*.

Utilize a Class

A typical approach for using a class is as follows:

```
local instance = class.new([…])
```
Creates and returns a new instance object of the class whose name is *class*.

```
class.method(instance[, …])
instance:method([…])
```
Calls the instance method named *method* on instance object *instance*, which was returned by a call to

class.new(). (Lua implicitly passes *instance* as the first argument to *method* when the character ':' is used instead of '.' when invoking *method*.)

```
function instance.method(self[, …]) block end
function instance:method([…])        block end
```

Defines a singleton method named *method* for instance object *instance*. *method* has a local variable named self that refers to *instance*.

If the class (or any superclasses) that *instance* belongs to also has an instance method named *method*, the method being defined overrides the existing method.

Modules

Lua has a simple system for creating and loading external *modules*. A module is basically a named collection of functions and variables (which may be constants). There are two types of modules: Lua modules and C modules. Lua modules are simply tables returned at the end of Lua source files. C modules are typically shared object binary files (e.g. *.so* or *.dll* files) and their contents are described in the section "C Modules" on page 124. Lua searches for modules within defined paths and can load them using the function require(), which is described in this section. Example 9 defines a simple Lua module for basic trigonometry that has degree and radian modes, and then uses that module, provided it is in Lua's module search path. The sub-section "Create a Lua Module" contains more information on the structure of Lua modules.

Numerous third-party modules supplied by Lua's vibrant community can be found and installed from the LuaRocks package manager.[7] Among them are: LuaSocket for working with sockets, LPeg for pattern matching with Parsing Expression Grammars (PEGs), LuaFileSystem for accessing the underlying filesystem, Penlight for a set of utilities inspired by Python's standard library, Luaposix for POSIX programming, Lapis for web development, and LuaUnit for unit testing.

7   https://luarocks.org/

Example 9. Define, load, and use a Lua module

```
-- File "trig.lua".
local M = {}

-- Radians mode.
M.rad = {
  sin = math.sin,
  cos = math.cos,
  tan = math.tan,
}

-- Degrees mode.
M.deg = {
  sin = function(x) return math.sin(math.rad(x)) end,
  cos = function(x) return math.cos(math.rad(x)) end,
  tan = function(x) return math.tan(math.rad(x)) end
}

return M

-- Program code.
local trig = require("trig").deg
trig.sin(30) -- results in 0.5
trig = require("trig").rad
trig.sin(math.pi / 6) -- also results in 0.5
```

package.path
package.cpath

> The string of ';'-delimited paths Lua searches for Lua
> modules and C modules in, with '?' characters represent-
> ing potential module names.

> The default paths are system-dependent and are config-
> urable when compiling Lua.

> The environment variables LUA_PATH, LUA_PATH_5_2, LUA_PA
> TH_5_3, LUA_PATH_5_4, LUA_CPATH, LUA_CPATH_5_2, LUA_CPATH_
> 5_3, and LUA_CPATH_5_4 control the initial value of Lua's
> package paths. If more than one of these environment
> variables are defined, priority is given to the versioned
> variable.

require(*name*)

> Searches package.path and package.cpath for the module
> whose string name is *name*, and loads and returns that
> module or, if no module was found, raises an error. Each

'.' character in *name* is treated as a directory separator.

If the module found is a Lua module, its contents are executed as a chunk of Lua code and the first value returned by that chunk is considered as the module to be returned. If the module found is a C module, its entry point function, `luaopen_name`, is called (with any '.' characters replaced by '_' and any "*-version*" suffix ignored), and the first value returned by that function is considered as the module to be returned. The section "C Modules" on page 124 describes C modules and their entry point functions in more detail.

In Lua 5.4, the first time a module is loaded, `require()` returns a second value that indicates how or where the module was found (e.g. `"path/to/name.lua"`).

Subsequent calls to `require()` with *name* will produce the original value returned, without reloading the module.

`package.loaded[name] = nil`
Unregisters the module whose string name is *name*.

A subsequent call to `require()` with *name* will reload the module.

`package.searchpath(name, paths[, sep[, repl]])`   Lua 5.2, 5.3, 5.4
Searches each ';'-delimited path in string *paths* for a file that exists whose filename is the one constructed by replacing each occurrence of '?' in the search path with string *name*, and returns the first found file's string filename. (Any instances of string *sep* in *name* are replaced with string *repl* first.) If no file was found, returns `nil` followed by an error message that lists all filenames tried. The default values of *sep* and *repl* are `"."` and `"/"`, respectively.

TIP

This function is not restricted for use by Lua's module system. It can be used for any purpose that involves finding a file in a set of directories.

Create a Lua Module

Lua modules do not have a defined structure other than they should return a table. A module can be a collection of functions, a set of configuration fields, or even a class. (Classes are described in the section "Define a Class" on page 38). As a result, there are many different approaches for writing modules. (One of them is shown in Example 9 on page 43.) Regardless of the approach, modules should avoid creating any global variables and should define only local or module variables. The typical "building blocks" for a module are as follows:

`local M = {}`
> Creates a new table that represents a module. The name of a module's table is traditionally M, since a module's actual name is based on the name of the Lua file it is in.

`M.variable = expr`
> Evaluates expression *expr* and assigns the resulting value to the module variable named *variable*.

`function M.name([…]) block end`
> Defines the module function named *name*.

`return M`
> Designates M as the value returned by the call to `require()` that loaded the module.

Legacy modules

Lua 5.1's method for creating modules centers around the function `module()`. However, that function was deprecated in Lua 5.2, so the table scheme in the preceding section should be used instead.

`module(name[, package.seeall])`   **Lua 5.1**
> Creates a new module whose string name is *name*, defines it as a global variable, and changes the global environment of the module to be the module itself. If the argument value `package.seeall` is given, the module's environment will inherit from the original global environment. (The next section, "Environments," describes what it means to change the global environment.)

> Each '.' character in *name* acts as a namespace separator.

Lua will ensure there are separate tables for each name-space. For example, the statement "`module("lua.qui ck.reference")`" creates the new module in the field `ref erence` of the field `quick` of the global table `lua`.

Environments

Technically, Lua's global variables are really non-local variables stored in an *environment* table, and Lua allows this table to be changed at any time. When retrieving the value of a non-local variable named *name*, Lua looks for the field *name* in the current environment table. Similarly, when assigning a value to a non-local variable, Lua creates the applicable key-value pair in the current environment.

By default, the current environment table is the global environment, `_G` (which also contains all of Lua's built-in functions and standard library modules). Thus, non-local variables can be considered global variables. When retrieving the value of the global variable `a`, Lua returns the value assigned to `_G.a`, and when assigning a value `b` to `a`, Lua executes the statement "`_G.a = b`". If the current environment is changed to another table, non-local variable access and assignment will operate using that table instead of `_G`.

As noted in the section "Variables and Scopes" on page 10, Lua's "globals by default" approach can lead to subtle bugs due to negligence. Example 10 primitively demonstrates how to overload table indexing and assignment in `_G` in order to catch undefined global variable access and prevent accidental global variable creation. The section "Other Operator and Statement Metamethods" on page 35 covers the metamethods used in this example.

Example 10. Control global variable access and assignment

```
setmetatable(_G, {
  __index = function(t, key)
    local errmsg = "Unknown global '%s'"
    error(string.format(errmsg, key))
  end,
```

```
__newindex = function(t, key, value)
  local errmsg = "Attempt to create global '%s'. \z
                Use rawset() instead."
  error(string.format(errmsg, key))
end
})
```

_G

The global environment table.

NOTE

Reassigning or deleting _G does not affect the global environment. Deleting values from or adding values to _G
does.

_ENV   Lua 5.2, 5.3, 5.4

The current environment table. Unless previously set, de-
faults to _G.

getfenv(*f*)   Lua 5.1
getfenv([*level*])   Lua 5.1

Returns the environment table for function *f* or the function at level number *level*. Level 1 refers to the current
function (or the current file or module if there is no current function), 2 refers to the caller of the current function, and so on. Level 0 refers to the global environment.
The default value of *level* is 1.

_ENV = *t*   Lua 5.2, 5.3, 5.4

Designates table *t* as the current environment within the
current block starting after the point of declaration and
within any sub-blocks. The environment outside the current block is unaffected.

setfenv(*f*, *t*)   Lua 5.1
setfenv(*level*, *t*)   Lua 5.1

Designates table *t* as the environment for function *f* or
the function at level number *level*. Level 1 refers to the
current function (or the current file or module if there is
no current function), 2 refers to the caller of the current
function, and so on. Level 0 refers to the global environment.

Error Handling and Warnings

Lua provides basic error handling facilities. Whenever Lua raises an error (either on its own or from an explicit instruction), it returns to the host program for handling unless the error occurs within a *protected call*. A protected call catches and handles errors from within Lua itself. The functions `pcall()` and `xpcall()` described in this section are protected calls, as is `coroutine.resume()`, which is described in the section "Start, Resume, and Yield a Thread" on page 71. Example 11 demonstrates how to handle errors raised when attempting to decode a text file's contents with an external, third-party function.

Errors normally have defined handlers. For the times when this is not the case (e.g. while closing to-be-closed variables, and during garbage collection), Lua 5.4 introduces the ability to emit warnings. However, the host is not required to follow this convention.

Example 11. Handle string encoding errors

```lua
local encodings = {
  "UTF-8", "UTF-16", "UTF-32", "ASCII", "ISO-8859-1"
}
local f = io.open(filename, "r")
local text = f:read("a")
f:close()
for i = 1, #encodings do
  -- Attempt to convert file contents to UTF-8.
  local ok, conv = pcall(toutf8, text, encodings[i])
  if ok then
    text = conv
    goto encoding_detected
  end
end
error("Could not detect file encoding.")
::encoding_detected::
--[[ process UTF-8-encoded text ]]
```

pcall (*f*[, *arg1*, *arg2*, …, *argN*])
xpcall(*f*, *error_handler*[, *arg1*, *arg2*, …, *argN*]) **Lua 5.2, 5.3, 5.4**
xpcall(*f*, *error_handler*) **Lua 5.1**

    Calls function *f* with argument values *arg1*, *arg2*, …, *argN*, and returns `true` if an error did not occur, followed by all of the values returned by *f*. Otherwise, returns `false` followed by an error message, which in the case of `xpcall()` is the value returned by function *error_han dler* (which was passed the original error message as a function argument).

`error(message[, level])`
Raises an error at level number *level* with string *message* as the error message. *level* indicates where in the call stack the error should be reported at. A level of `1` implicates the current function (or the current file or module if there is no current function), `2` implicates the caller of the current function, and so on. A level of `0` omits call stack information. The default value of *level* is `1`.

NOTE

message can be any Lua value, not just a string. (For example, an error could be reported as a table that contains a numeric error code and string message.) However, since Lua itself only raises errors with string messages, and for the sake of simplicity, this book refers to all error values as error message strings.

`assert(expr[, message])`
Asserts that expression *expr* evaluates to boolean true (i.e. not `false` or `nil`), and returns all values returned by *expr*. Otherwise, raises an error with string *message* as the error message, which is `"assertion failed!"` by default.

TIP

The statement "`assert(expr, message)`" is a shortcut for "`if not expr then error(message) end`".

`warn(message[, …])`   Lua 5.4
Emits a warning message composed of the concatenation of all string arguments given. If *message* is `"@off"` or `"@on"`, warning emission is turned off or on, respectively.

By default, warnings are printed to `io.stderr`. The section "Error and Warning Handling" on page 129 describes how a host program can alter this behavior.

Load and Run Dynamic Code

Lua can load and execute user-provided chunks of Lua code at run-time. It can also do this in a sandboxed environment as a security measure. Example 12 demonstrates how to safely execute the contents of a sample configuration file and store all key-value assignments in a table for processing.

Example 12. Safely load a configuration file

```
-- File "config.lua".
width = 600
height = 400
home_path = "/home/mitchell"

-- Program code.
local config = {}
assert(loadfile("config.lua", "t", config))()
for option, setting in pairs(config) do
  --[[ process option and setting... ]]
end
```

dofile([*filename*])
> Executes as a chunk of Lua code the contents of the file identified by string *filename* or io.stdin and returns all values returned by that chunk.

load (*chunk*[, *name*[, *mode*[, *env*]]])	**Lua 5.2, 5.3, 5.4**
loadstring(*chunk*[, *name*])	**Lua 5.1**
loadfile ([*filename*[, *mode*[, *env*]]])	**Lua 5.2, 5.3, 5.4**
loadfile ([*filename*])	**Lua 5.1**

> Loads as a chunk of Lua code string *chunk* or the contents of the file identified by string *filename* or io.stdin and returns a function that will execute that chunk when called, within environment *env*. *name* is an optional string name associated with the chunk and is used in error messages. String *mode* indicates whether the chunk can be text ("t"), binary ("b"), or both ("bt"), and its default value is "bt". (Binary chunks are produced by Lua's *luac* or *luac.exe* executable.) The section "Environments" on page 46 describes environments.

> If the chunk contains a syntax error, nil is returned followed by an error message.

> *chunk* may also be a function that, when repeatedly

called, returns strings to be concatenated into a single
chunk (a blank string or `nil` signals the end of the
chunk).

CAUTION

Lua does not verify the integrity of, or in any way sanitize
binary chunks. Running truly arbitrary binary chunks may
be unsafe.

Numeric Facilities

Lua's math module, `math`, provides basic numeric functions
and constants.

NOTE

Lua 5.3 removed a few previously available mathematical
functions related to subjects like hyperbolic trigonometry
and float decomposition. Those functions (along with
other useful ones) are available in an external module
maintained by one of Lua's authors.[8]

`math.sqrt(x)`
> Returns the square root of number *x*.

`math.abs(x)`
> Returns the absolute value of number *x*.

`math.ceil (x)`
`math.floor(x)`
> Returns number *x* rounded up or down to the nearest in-
> teger.

`math.min(…)`
`math.max(…)`
> Returns the least or greatest of the argument values
> given.

`math.fmod(x, y)`
> Returns the remainder of *x* / *y* that rounds the quotient
> towards zero. (By contrast, the modulo (%) operator
> rounds towards minus infinity.)

8   *http://webserver2.tecgraf.puc-rio.br/~lhf/ftp/lua/#lmathx*

`math.modf(x)`
>   Returns the integral and fractional parts of number *x*.

`math.huge`
>   A value greater than any other numeric Lua value (typically the special float value that represents infinity).

Trigonometric Functions

Lua can do basic trigonometry.

`math.pi`
>   The value of the constant π.

`math.sin(x)`
`math.cos(x)`
`math.tan(x)`
>   Returns the sine, cosine, or tangent of number *x*, which is in radians.

`math.asin(x)`
`math.acos(x)`
`math.atan(x)`   **Lua 5.1, 5.2**
>   Returns, in radians, the arc sine, arc cosine, or arc tangent of number *x*.

`math.atan(y[, x])`   **Lua 5.3, 5.4**
`math.atan2(y, x)`   **Lua 5.1, 5.2**
>   Returns, in radians, the arc tangent of *y* / *x* in the proper quadrant. *x* can be 0 and its default value is 1.

`math.sinh(x)`   **Lua 5.1, 5.2**
`math.cosh(x)`   **Lua 5.1, 5.2**
`math.tanh(x)`   **Lua 5.1, 5.2**
>   Returns the hyperbolic sine, cosine, or tangent of number *x*.

`math.rad(x)`
`math.deg(x)`
>   Returns number *x* converted from degrees to radians and vice-versa.

Exponential and Logarithmic Functions

Lua can work with exponentials and logarithms.

```
math.exp(x)
```
Returns e^x.

```
math.log(x[, base])
```                                              **Lua 5.2, 5.3, 5.4**
```
math.log(x)
```                                                          **Lua 5.1**
Returns the logarithm of number x in base number *base*.
The default value of *base* is e.

```
math.log10(x)
```                                                        **Lua 5.1**
Returns the base-10 logarithm of number x.

Generate Random Numbers

Lua can generate pseudo-random numbers.

```
math.randomseed([x[, y]])
```                                          **Lua 5.4**
```
math.randomseed(x)
```                                      **Lua 5.1, 5.2, 5.3**
Reinitializes the pseudo-random number generator with
a seed produced from integers x and y. Identical seeds
generate identical sequences of pseudo-random numbers. In Lua 5.4, if x and y are not given, they are gener-
ated, used, and returned.

TIP

In Lua 5.1, 5.2, and 5.3, the random number generator is
always initialized with the same seed. The statement
"`math.randomseed(os.time())`" can be used to generate different sets of random numbers each time a program runs,
provided the run frequency is no more than once per
second.

```
math.random()
```
Returns a pseudo-random float in the range [0, 1).

```
math.random([m, ]n)
```
Returns a pseudo-random integer between m and n, inclusive. The default value of m is 1.

In Lua 5.4, if n is 0 and m is not given, a pseudo-random
integer in the range [`math.mininteger`, `math.maxinteger`] is
returned.

Work with Integers

Lua 5.3 introduced some features related to its new ability to represent numbers internally as integers.

math.type(x)   Lua 5.3, 5.4
Returns "integer" if value *x* is a number whose internal representation is an integer, "float" if *x* is a number whose internal representation is a float, or nil if *x* is not a number.

math.tointeger(x)   Lua 5.3, 5.4
Returns number *x* converted to an integer, or nil if the conversion fails.

math.ult(m, n)   Lua 5.3, 5.4
Returns whether or not integer *m* is less than integer *n* when compared as unsigned integers.

math.mininteger   Lua 5.3, 5.4
math.maxinteger   Lua 5.3, 5.4
The least and greatest possible integer values Lua can represent (typically -2^{63} and 2^{63}, respectively). Integers wrap on overflow or underflow.

String Facilities

Lua's string modules, string and utf8, contain tools for creating compound strings, querying and transforming strings, searching and replacing within strings, and working with UTF-8-encoded strings. These modules operate under the premise that byte positions in strings start at 1 (not 0, as in C). Byte positions may be negative, which indicates string functions will count from the end of the string. With the aid of the string module, string values also behave like objects (e.g. the expression "s:lower()" is equivalent to "string.lower(s)"). The following sections cover Lua's string modules.

Create a Compound String

In addition to the quote and bracket syntax for creating simple strings, Lua provides some convenience functions for creating compound strings, including formatted strings. Tables 4 and 5 list the flags and specifiers available for formatted strings.

Table 4. String formatting flags

Character	Meaning
+ or ' ' (space)	Display a '+' sign or leading space, respectively, in front of positive numbers.
- or 0	Left-align or pad with leading zeros, respectively, a placeholder's value.
#	Always display a decimal point and do not truncate trailing zeros for floats, or display a leading '0x' or '0' for hexadecimal and octal numbers, respectively.

Table 5. String formatting specifiers

Character	Argument Value Type	Meaning
d, i	Integer	Decimal integer
u	Integer	Unsigned decimal integer
x, X	Integer	Hexadecimal integer
o	Integer	Octal integer
f, F	Float	Decimal float
e, E	Float	Exponential notation float
g, G	Float	The shorter of decimal or exponential notation float
a, A	Float	Hexadecimal float
c	Integer	Character byte
s	String	String
p[a]	Any	Hexadecimal address
q	String	Safely-quoted Lua string
%	N/A	Literal '%'

[a] Only in Lua 5.4.

`string.format(format, …)`
    Returns a formatted version of the argument values

given, subject to string *format*. *format* contains a sequence of placeholders that specify how to format their respective values. Each placeholder has the following syntax:

`%[flags][field_width][.precision]specifier`

Table 4 lists valid flags for *flags* along with their meanings. *field_width* specifies the minimum number of characters used to display a placeholder's value. *precision* indicates the minimum number of digits to display (including leading zeros) for integers, the minimum number of decimal places to display for floats, and the minimum number of bytes to display for strings. Table 5 lists valid specifiers for *specifier* along with their meanings.

`string.rep(s, n[, separator])`   **Lua 5.2, 5.3, 5.4**
`string.rep(s, n)`   **Lua 5.1**
Returns a string composed of *n* of concatenations of string *s* separated by string *separator*. The default value of *separator* is the empty string.

`table.concat(t[, separator[, i[, j]]])`
Returns the string concatenation of all elements in list *t* between indices *i* and *j*, inclusive, separated by string *separator*. The default value of *separator* is the empty string, and the default values of *i* and *j* are 1 and #t, respectively.

Example 16 on page 67 illustrates how to efficiently pretty print the contents of a table.

`string.char(…)`
Returns a string composed of characters whose byte values are the argument values given.

Create and work with a binary string

Lua 5.3 introduced the ability to create and work with binary strings packed with structured data. Table 6 lists the options available for specifying data to pack. The data types for many of those options are C data types. Example 13 demonstrates how data from a game might be saved in a simple, unencrypted binary format.

Table 6. Conversion options for packed strings

Option	Meaning	Option	Meaning
<	Little endian	T	size_t
>	Big endian	i[*n*]	Integer of *n* bytes[c]
=	Native endian[a]	I[*n*]	Unsigned integer of *n* bytes[c]
![*n*]	Maximum alignment of *n*[b, c]	f	float
b	char	d	double
B	unsigned char	n	lua_Number
h	short	c*n*	String of *n* bytes
H	unsigned short	z	Zero-terminated string
l (lower-case 'L')	long	s[*n*]	String preceded by its byte length as an integer of *n* bytes[c]
L	unsigned long	x	Padding byte (0)
j	lua_Integer	X*op*	Empty version of option *op* for alignment padding
J	lua_Unsigned	' ' (space)	Ignored

[a] This is the default endian. It assumes the whole system is either big or little endian.

[b] The default value is 1. An alignment of *n* ensures that for the length of the string, there is a data value starting at every byte multiple of *n* (unless that data value's size is larger than *n*). This does not mean every data value starts at a multiple of *n*. Values are padded as necessary in order to ensure alignment.

[c] *n* is optional, but must be between 1 and 16.

Example 13. Save game data in a binary format

```
-- Saved player data comprises a name, level (0-100),
-- attribute stats (0-255), map xy-coordinate position,
-- and item inventory preceded by inventory size.
-- Inventory items each have an id (0-65535) and count
-- (0-255).
```

```lua
local info_fmt = "zI1"
local stats_fmt = "I1I1"
local position_fmt = "ii"
local inventory_item_fmt = "I2I1"

function save_player_data(player)
  -- Generate static player save data.
  local data = {
    info_fmt:pack(player.name, player.level),
    stats_fmt:pack(player.strength, player.defense),
    position_fmt:pack(player.x, player.y),
    string.pack("I1", #player.inventory)
  }
  -- Generate dynamic player save data.
  for i = 1, #player.inventory do
    local item = player.inventory[i]
    data[#data + 1] = string.pack(inventory_item_fmt,
                                  item.id, item.count)
  end
  data = table.concat(data)
  --[[ save data... ]]
end

function load_player_data(player)
  --[[ read data... ]]
  local name, level, stats, x, y, inventory_size, pos
  -- Read static player save data.
  name, level, pos = info_fmt:unpack(data)
  stats = {stats_fmt:unpack(data, pos)}
  x, y, pos = position_fmt:unpack(data, stats[3])
  -- Read dynamic player save data.
  inventory_size, pos = string.unpack("I1", data, pos)
  local inventory = {}
  for i = 1, inventory_size do
    local id, ct
    id, ct, pos = inventory_item_fmt:unpack(data, pos)
    inventory[#inventory + 1] = {id = id, count = ct}
  end
  -- Load player data.
  player.name, player.level = name, level
  player.strength, player.defense = stats[1], stats[2]
  player.x, player.y = x, y
  player.inventory = inventory
end
```

`string.pack(`*`format,`* `…)`   **Lua 5.3, 5.4**
> Returns a serialized, binary string version of the argument values given, subject to string *format*. Table 6 lists the options available for serializing values.

`string.packsize(`*`format`*`)`   **Lua 5.3, 5.4**
> Returns the number of bytes in any serialized, binary string constructed from string *format*, which cannot contain the 'z' or 's' options. Table 6 lists the options available for serializing values.

`string.unpack(`*`format,`* `s[,` *`init`*`])`   **Lua 5.3, 5.4**
> Returns, subject to string *format* (and ignoring padding bytes), the unserialized values in binary string *s* starting at byte position *init*, and also returns the position in *s* after the last returned value.

Query and Transform Strings

Strings can be queried and transformed. However, since strings are immutable, the results from string transformations are new strings.

`string.sub(s, i[, j])`
> Returns the substring of string *s* between byte positions *i* and *j*, inclusive. The default value of *j* is -1.

`string.byte(s[, i[, j]])`
> Returns the byte values of the characters in string *s* between byte positions *i* and *j*, inclusive. The default values for *i* and *j* are 1 and *i*, respectively.

`string.len(s)`
> Returns the number of bytes in string *s*, including embedded zeros. Equivalent to the expression "`#s`".

`string.lower(s)`
`string.upper(s)`
> Returns a copy of string *s* with all upper-case letters converted to lower-case or all lower-case letters converted to upper-case, according to the current locale.

`string.reverse(s)`
> Returns a copy of *s* with its bytes reversed.

Search and Replace Within a String

Lua's searching and replacing facilities for strings are unique, yet powerful. Due to size and memory considerations, Lua does not support regular expressions (regex). Instead, Lua has its own pattern-matching language that is very small, remarkably fast, and extremely efficient. Search strings that utilize this language are called *patterns*. Table 7 lists Lua's pattern syntax and Example 14 exhibits many of Lua's pattern capabilities with a simple URL parser.

TIP

Patterns that use anchors ('^' and/or '$') match text much more quickly than patterns without anchors.

Example 14. Simple URL parser

```lua
function urlparse(url)
  -- Decode escapes like "%5C" -> "\".
  url = url:gsub("%%(%x%x)", function(c)
    return string.char(tonumber(c, 16))
  end)
  -- Parse out URL parts.
  local patt = "^([^:]+)://([^/]+)(.*)$"
  local scheme, host_part, rest = url:match(patt)
  local host, port = host_part:match("^([^:]+):?
(%d*)")
  local path, query = rest:match("^([^?]*)%??(.*)$")
  local parts = {}
  for part in query:gmatch("[^&]+") do
    local k, v = part:match("^([^=]+)=(.*)$")
    parts[k] = v
  end
  -- Return parsed parts in a table.
  return {
    scheme = scheme,
    host = host, port = tonumber(port) or 80,
    path = path, query = parts
  }
end

urlparse("http://www.example.com/path?key=value")
-- results in:
-- {scheme = "http", host = "www.example.com",
--   port = 80, path = "/path", query = {key = "value"}}
```

Table 7. Pattern syntax

Characters	Meaning
.	Matches any character.
%a or %A	Matches any letter or its complement, respectively.
%c or %C	Matches any control character or its complement, respectively.
%d or %D	Matches any digit or its complement, respectively.
%g or %G	Matches any printable character except space or matches its complement, respectively. (Not in Lua 5.1.)
%l or %L	Matches any lower-case letter or its complement, respectively.
%p or %P	Matches any punctuation character or its complement, respectively.
%s or %S	Matches any space character or its complement, respectively.
%u or %U	Matches any upper-case character or its complement, respectively.
%w or %W	Matches any alphanumeric character or its complement, respectively.
%x or %X	Matches any hexadecimal digit or its complement, respectively.
%z or %Z	Matches an embedded zero or its complement, respectively. (Only in Lua 5.1, which cannot handle '\0'.)
[set] or [^set]	Matches any character in *set* (including ranges like [A-Za-z]) or its complement, respectively.
*	Matches the previous *character class* zero or more times. The character sequences listed previously in this table are character classes.
+	Matches the previous class one or more times.
-	Matches the previous class zero or more times, but as few times as possible.
?	Matches the previous class once, or not at all.
%b*xy*	Matches a balanced range that starts with *x* and ends with *y*.
%f[*set*]	Matches a position where the next character belongs to *set*, but the previous character does not.

Characters	Meaning
^ or $	Matches the beginning or end of a line, respectively, unless inside a set.
(*pattern*)	Matches pattern *pattern* and captures its text. An empty pattern captures the current position.
%*n*	Matches the nth captured pattern's text.
%*x*	Matches non-alphanumeric character *x* literally, ignoring any special meaning it may have by itself.

string.find(*s, pattern*[, *init*[, *plain*]])
> Searches string *s* for pattern *pattern* starting at byte position *init*, and returns the start and end byte positions of the match followed by any string values captured by *pattern* or, if no match was found, returns nil. The default value of *init* is 1. *plain* is a flag that indicates whether or not to treat *pattern* as a literal string instead of a pattern, and its default value is false.

string.gmatch(*s, pattern*[, *init*])   **Lua 5.4**
string.gmatch(*s, pattern*)   **Lua 5.1, 5.2, 5.3**
> Returns an iterator that can be used in a for loop to iterate over all occurrences of pattern *pattern* in string *s* starting at byte position *init*. The default value of *init* is 1. If *pattern* has captures, the captured values are assigned to loop variables. Otherwise, the entire match is used.

string.gsub(*s, pattern, replacement*[, *n*])
> Returns a copy of string s where all (or the first *n*) instances of pattern *pattern* are replaced by string *replacement*, and also returns the number of replacements made. *replacement* may contain "%*d*" sequences, which represent the dth value captured by *pattern* ("%0" represents the entire match).

> *replacement* may also be a table or function. If it is a table and the match or first capture exists as a key, that key's associated value is used as the replacement text. If *replacement* is a function, that function is called with either the captured values or the entire match passed as arguments. If the function returns a string or number, that value is used as the replacement text.

`string.match(s, pattern[, init])`
> Searches string *s* for pattern *pattern* starting at byte position *init*, and returns either the values captured by *pattern* or the entire match itself or, if no match was found, returns `nil`. The default value of *init* is `1`.

Work with UTF-8 Strings

Lua 5.3 introduced some basic utilities for creating and working with strings that contain UTF-8-encoded characters. (These utilities truly are basic, since more extensive support for UTF-8 is too complicated for a small, simple language like Lua.) UTF-8 is a universally accepted and widely-used encoding for strings that is compatible with ASCII. Whereas ASCII characters are single bytes, UTF-8 characters may be multiple bytes in length. Despite this, most of the functions in Lua's `utf8` module still operate on byte positions, not character positions.

`utf8.char(…)`   **Lua 5.3, 5.4**
> Returns a string composed of UTF-8 characters whose numeric codepoints are the argument values given.

`utf8.codepoint(s[, i[, j[, lax]]])`   **Lua 5.4**
`utf8.codepoint(s[, i[, j]])`   **Lua 5.3**
> Returns the numeric codepoints of the valid UTF-8 characters in string *s* that start between byte positions *i* and *j*, inclusive. The default values of *i* and *j* are `1` and *i*, respectively. *lax* is a flag that indicates whether or not to include codepoints for invalid UTF-8 characters, and its default value is `false`.

`utf8.len(s[, i[, j[, lax]]])`   **Lua 5.4**
`utf8.len(s[, i[, j]])`   **Lua 5.3**
> Returns the number of valid UTF-8 characters in string *s* that start between byte positions *i* and *j*, inclusive. The default values of *i* and *j* are `1` and `-1`, respectively. *lax* is a flag that indicates whether or not to include invalid UTF-8 characters, and its default value is `false`. If *s* contains an invalid byte sequence, returns `false` followed by the byte position of the invalid byte.

```
utf8.codes(s[, lax])                                      Lua 5.4
utf8.codes(s)                                             Lua 5.3
```
Returns an iterator that can be used in a for loop to iterate over all pairs of byte positions and valid UTF-8 codepoints in string s. lax is a flag that indicates whether or not to include invalid UTF-8 codepoints, and its default value is false.

```
utf8.offset(s, n[, i])                               Lua 5.3, 5.4
```
Returns the byte position in string s of the nth UTF-8 character from byte position i, or nil if no character was found. The default value of i is 1 for non-negative n and #s + 1 for negative n.

```
utf8.charpattern                                     Lua 5.3, 5.4
```
A pattern that matches a single UTF-8 character in a string.

Table and List Facilities

Lua provides built-in functions for iterating over tables. It also supplies a table module, table, that (despite the name) contains tools for manipulating the contents of lists. The table module operates under the premise that its functions receive lists as argument values. A list is a special kind of table that has non-nil values assigned to integer keys from 1 to n where n is the number of elements in the list. (Lists may also have non-numeric keys, but those keys and their associated values are ignored by table.) Prior to Lua 5.3, table bypassed all metamethods. The following sections describe Lua's facilities for working with tables and lists.

Iterate Over a Table

Lua can iterate over tables and lists using a for loop. By nature tables (and lists) are unordered, regardless of the sequence in which key-value pairs were added to them and regardless of their logical order. However, there are methods for iterating over tables in a specific order, such as the one Example 15 demonstrates, which iterates over a table based on the order of its string keys.

NOTE

Modifying a table during traversal is permitted as long as no new key-value pairs are added. If a new pair is added, traversal must begin anew.

Example 15. Iterate over a table in order by string keys

```
-- Create the table to be iterated over.
local t = {a = 1, b = 2, c = 3, --[[...]] z = 26}

-- Create intermediate list of keys and sort it.
local keys = {}
for k, v in pairs(t) do
  keys[#keys + 1] = k
end
table.sort(keys)

-- Now iterate in key order.
for _, k in ipairs(keys) do
  local v = t[k]
  --[[ process v... ]]
end
```

pairs(t)

Returns an iterator that can be used in a **for** loop to iterate over all key-value pairs in table *t*. If *t* has the metamethod __pairs(), that metamethod is called to produce an iterator. The section "Function Metamethods" on page 37 covers this metamethod in its generic form.

Iteration order is not defined, even if *t* is a list.

ipairs(t)

Returns an iterator that can be used in a **for** loop to iterate over ordered index-element pairs in list *t*. In Lua 5.3 and 5.4, if *t* has the metafield __index or the metamethod __index(), that entity is used to produce the pairs. In Lua 5.2, if *t* has the metamethod __ipairs(), that meta-method is called to produce an iterator. The sections "Other Operator and Statement Metamethods" on page 35 and "Function Metamethods" on page 37 cover these respective cases. In Lua 5.1, iteration behavior cannot be altered.

Manipulate Lists

The contents of lists can be manipulated in-place.

`table.insert(t, [i, ]value)`
> Inserts value *value* into list *t* at index *i*, shifting subsequent elements towards the end of the list. The default value of *i* is `#t + 1`.

`table.remove(t[, i])`
> Removes from list *t* the value at index *i*, shifting subsequent elements towards the beginning of the list, and returns the removed value. The default value of *i* is `#t`.

`table.sort(t[, f])`
> Sorts the elements of list *t* in-place, subject to comparator function *f*. *f* is passed two list elements and should return `true` if the first element comes before the second. The default comparator is the "less than" operator.

`table.move(from, i, j, k[, to])`   Lua 5.3, 5.4
> Moves all elements between indices *i* and *j*, inclusive, from list *from* to list *to*, starting at index *k* in *to*. The default value of *to* is *from*.

Unpack Lists

Multiple elements can be extracted from a list for use in mul-

---

tiple variable assignment statements, multiple value return statements, function calls with multiple arguments, and table constructors.

table.unpack(*t*[, *i*[, *j*]])   **Lua 5.2, 5.3, 5.4**
unpack   (*t*[, *i*[, *j*]])   **Lua 5.1**
　　Returns the elements in list *t* between indices *i* and *j*, inclusive. The default values of *i* and *j* are 1 and #*t*, respectively.

Create Strings from Lists

Instead of concatenating a large number of individual strings together into one string, it is far more efficient to store the individual strings in a list and concatenate them all together at once (sometimes with a separator as well). Example 16 illustrates how to pretty print the contents of a table.

Example 16. Pretty print a table

```
-- Print something like "{a = 1, b = 2, c = 3}".
local items = {}
for k, v in pairs(t) do
  items[#items + 1] = string.format("%s = %s", k, v)
end
table.sort(items)
print(string.format("{%s}", table.concat(items, ",
")))
```

table.concat(*t*[, *separator*[, *i*[, *j*]]])
　　Returns the string concatenation of all elements in list *t* between indices *i* and *j*, inclusive, separated by string *separator*. The default value of *separator* is the empty string, and the default values of *i* and *j* are 1 and #*t*, respectively.

Thread Facilities

Lua's threading facilities are supplied by coroutines. Coroutines run independently from one another, but share the same global environment. However, unlike true multi-threading, only one coroutine can be active at a time. Coroutines work collaboratively by resuming one another and yielding to one another. The typical threading procedure is as follows:

1. The main Lua thread creates a new (suspended) thread *T* with a function body that does some work.

2. Upon starting *T*, the main thread is temporarily suspended, and the body of *T* is executed.

3. *T* performs some work and then yields back to the main thread.

4. The main thread resumes right where it left off, at the point where it started *T*. *T* is now suspended.

5. The main thread performs some work and then resumes *T*.

6. *T* resumes right where it left off, at the point where it yielded back to the main thread. The main thread is now suspended.

7. This process repeats until *T* completes its work and the thread finishes.

8. The main thread resumes right where it left off and continues indefinitely. *T* is now dead and cannot be resumed.

During each transition between threads, values can be exchanged. When the main thread starts *T*, it can pass values to the function body of *T*. When *T* yields, it can pass values back to the main thread. When the main thread resumes *T*, it can pass more values to *T*. And so on.

All of this is embodied in Example 17 and described in the following sections. Additionally, Example 18 illustrates how a thread can be used as an iterator in a `for` loop.

Example 17. Emulate `string.gsub()` without captures

```
-- Returns a thread that, for each instance of a
-- pattern found, yields that match to main thread and
-- substitutes it with the replacement received.
```

```
local function gsub(str, patt, init)
  init = init or 1
  return coroutine.create(function()
    local buffer = {} -- for building resultant string
    local s, e = str:find(patt, init)
    while s do
      -- Add substring up to match to result buffer.
      buffer[#buffer + 1] = str:sub(init, s - 1)
      -- Yield match, receive replacement, and add to
      -- result buffer.
      local match = str:sub(s, e)
      local replacement = coroutine.yield(match)
      buffer[#buffer + 1] = replacement
      -- Continue the search.
      init = e + 1
      s, e = str:find(patt, init)
    end
    -- Build and return the final replacement string.
    return table.concat(buffer)
  end)
end

-- Replaces all instances of a pattern in a string by
-- creating a thread that searches within that string
-- and, for each match yielded, produces a suitable
-- replacement.
local function threaded_gsub(str, patt)
  local thread = gsub(str, patt)
  local ok, match = coroutine.resume(thread)
  while coroutine.status(thread) == "suspended" do
    local replacement = --[[ produce from match... ]]
    ok, match = coroutine.resume(thread, replacement)
  end
  return match -- final resultant string
end
```

Example 18. Generate list permutations

```
-- Permutes a list by taking each element and
-- recursively re-ordering the remaining elements.
-- For instance, given {1, 2, 3}:
-- Takes 1 and re-orders 2 and 3 (1, 2, 3 and 1, 3, 2).
-- Takes 2 and re-orders 1 and 3 (2, 1, 3 and 2, 3, 1).
-- Takes 3 and re-orders 1 and 2 (3, 1, 2 and 3, 2, 1).
local function permute(list, i)
  i = i or 1
  if i > #list then
```

```lua
      coroutine.yield(list)
    else
      for j = i, #list do
        list[i], list[j] = list[j], list[i]
        permute(list, i + 1)
        list[i], list[j] = list[j], list[i]
      end
    end
end

-- Iterator.
local function permutations(list)
  return coroutine.wrap(function() permute(list) end)
end

for permutation in permutations{1, 2, 3} do
  --[[ process permutation... ]]
end
```

Create a Thread

Threads can be created in one of two ways.

coroutine.create(*f*)
> Creates and returns a suspended thread with function *f* as its body.

coroutine.wrap(*f*)
> Creates a new thread with function *f* as its body and returns a function that, when called, starts or resumes that thread. The first time the returned function is called, the argument values passed to it are passed as arguments to the thread's function body. In subsequent calls, arguments passed are used as the return values of the call to coroutine.yield() that originally yielded the thread.
>
> If the thread subsequently yields without error, the function call returns the argument values passed to the yielding coroutine.yield() call. If the thread finishes without error, the function call returns the values returned by the thread's function body. Any errors that occur are not handled by the returned function.

Start, Resume, and Yield a Thread

Threads can be started, resumed, and yielded.

`coroutine.resume(thread[, val1, val2, …, valN])`
> Starts or resumes the execution of thread *thread* with values *val1*, *val2*, …, *valN* as arguments. If *thread* is being started, those values are passed as arguments to the thread's function body. If *thread* is being resumed, those values are used as the return values of the call to `corou tine.yield()` that originally yielded *thread*.
>
> If *thread* subsequently yields without error, this function returns `true` followed by the argument values passed to the yielding `coroutine.yield()` call. If *thread* finishes without error, this function returns `true` followed by the values returned by the thread's function body. If an error does occur, this function returns `false` followed by the error message.

`coroutine.isyieldable([thread])`   **Lua 5.4**
`coroutine.isyieldable()`   **Lua 5.3**
> Returns whether or not thread *thread* or the running thread can yield.

`coroutine.yield([…])`
> Suspends execution of the current thread, using any argument values given as the (potentially extra) return values of the call that originally started or resumed this thread.
>
> In Lua 5.1, threads cannot be suspended when a C function, metamethod, or iterator is active.

Query Thread Status

Threads can be queried for their current status.

`coroutine.status(thread)`
> Returns the string status of thread *thread*: `"running"` if the thread is running, `"suspended"` if the thread has not yet started or has yielded, `"normal"` if the thread is active but not running (i.e. it called `coroutine.resume()` on another thread), or `"dead"` if the thread has finished (whether normally, due to an error, or via `coroutine.close()`).

```
coroutine.running()
```
   Returns the running thread followed by a flag that indicates whether or not that thread is the main thread. If the main thread is running in Lua 5.1, returns `nil` instead.

Close a Thread

Threads can be closed in Lua 5.4, although this is typically only done when a thread has variables that need to be closed and either that thread is suspended and not expected to be resumed, or an error has occurred inside of it.

```
coroutine.close(thread)
```
                                                              Lua 5.4
   Closes thread *thread* and its to-be-closed variables and returns `true` if no error occurred during the closing process. Otherwise, returns `false` and an error message.

Input and Output Facilities

Lua's input and output module, `io`, contains tools for reading and writing to files and processes. Lua's operating system module, `os`, supplies some simple tools for managing files. Table 8 lists the modes Lua can open files in and Table 9 lists the formats available for reading data in. When it comes to reading and writing files, Lua provides two different models: the simple model, and the object-oriented model. Each of these models are described in the following sections, as is how to manage files and interact with processes.

Table 8. File open modes

Mode	Description
"r"	Read-only
"w"	Write-only (contents erased)
"a"	Append only
"r+"	Read and write
"w+"	Read and write (contents erased)
"a+"	Read and append

Mode	Description
"rb", "wb", "ab", "r+b", "w+b", "a+b"	For opening binary files

Table 9. Read formats

Format	Description	Return Value
number	Read *number* bytes	String, or `nil` on end of file (EOF)
"*n", "n"[a]	Read a number	Number, or `nil` if the conversion fails
"*l", "l"[a]	Read a line, skipping over the end of line (EOL) character(s)	String, or `nil` on EOF
"*L"[b], "L"[a]	Read a line with the EOL character(s)	String, or `nil` on EOF
"*a", "a"[a]	Read the remainder of the file	String (empty on EOF)

[a] Not in Lua 5.1 or 5.2.
[b] Not in Lua 5.1.

Simple Input and Output

Lua's simple input and output model consists of designating a filename as the file to read from and designating another filename as the file to write to. Subsequent calls to functions in Lua's `io` module will interact with the designated files. By default, the file to read from is standard input (stdin) and the file to write to is standard output (stdout). Example 19 demonstrates something akin to the UNIX tool *grep*, but with Lua patterns instead.

Example 19. Echo lines matching a Lua pattern

```
local date_patt = "%d+/%d+/%d+"
local line = io.read("*L")
while line do
  if line:find(date_patt) then
    io.write(line)
  end
  line = io.read("*L")
end
-- Note: for line in io.lines(io.stdin, "*L") do … end
```

```
-- is also valid.
```

io.input(*filename*)
io.input(*file*)
> Designates the file identified by string *filename* or file
> *file* to be the current input file.

io.read([...])
> Reads and returns values read from the current input file
> according to the formats specified by the argument val-
> ues given or, if an error occurred, returns nil followed
> by the error message. Table 9 lists the available formats.
> If no formats are specified, "l" is used in Lua 5.3 and
> 5.4, while "*l" is used in Lua 5.1 and 5.2.

TIP

If there is still data to read, the expression "io.read(0)"
returns the empty string without reading anything.

---

io.output(*filename*)
io.output(*file*)
> Designates the file identified by string *filename* or file
> *file* to be the current output file.

io.write(...)
> Writes the string or number argument values given to the
> current output file and returns that file or, if an error oc-
> curred, returns nil followed by the error message.

io.flush()
> Saves any unwritten, buffered data to the current output
> file.

io.close([*file*])
> Closes file *file* or the current output file, saving any un-
> written, buffered data to it.

io.lines([*filename*[, ...]])   **Lua 5.2, 5.3, 5.4**
io.lines([*filename*])   **Lua 5.1**
> Returns an iterator that can be used in a **for** loop to iter-
> ate over all lines in the file identified by string *filename*
> or the current input file. Each line is read according to
> the formats specified by the extra argument values given,
> and the resulting values are assigned to loop variables.
> Table 9 lists the available formats. If no formats are spec-

ified, "l" is used in Lua 5.3 and 5.4, while "*l" is used in
Lua 5.1 and 5.2.

io.input ()
io.output()
Returns the current input and output file, which, by default, are io.stdin and io.stdout, respectively.

Object-Oriented Input and Output

Lua's object-oriented input and output model consists of
opening a file, obtaining a file handle for that opened file,
and using that handle to interact with the file. Example 20 illustrates how to obtain a file's size in bytes.

Example 20. Obtain a file's size before processing it

```
local f = io.open(filename, "r")
local size = f:seek("end")
f:seek("set") -- restore position to beginning of file
```

io.open(*filename*[, *mode*])
Opens the file identified by string *filename* in string
mode *mode*, and returns a file handle or, if an error occurred, returns nil followed by the error message. Table
8 lists the available modes for opening files in. The default value for *mode* is "r".

io.stdin
io.stdout
io.stderr
Files that represent the host's standard input, standard
output, and standard error streams.

io.tmpfile()
Creates a temporary file and returns a file handle for
reading and writing to that file. The returned file is
deleted when the program ends.

os.tmpname()
Returns the string name of a file that can be opened,
written to, and used as a temporary file (e.g. in a shell
command).

For security reasons, on POSIX systems the returned filename is actually created and must be explicitly removed.

On Windows, the returned filename is just a base name and does not include the path to the system's temporary directory. The expression "os.getenv("TEMP")" returns that path.

file:read([…])
> Reads and returns values read from file *file* according to the formats specified by the argument values given or, if an error occurred, returns nil followed by the error message. Table 9 lists the available formats. If no formats are specified, "l" is used in Lua 5.3 and 5.4, while "*l" is used in Lua 5.1 and 5.2.

TIP

If there is still data to read, the expression "*file*:read(0)" returns the empty string without reading anything.

---

file:seek(["cur"])
> Returns the current byte position in file *file*.

file:seek("set"[, *offset*])
> Sets the current byte position in file *file* to *offset* (measured from the beginning of *file*) and returns that position. The default value of *offset* is 0.

file:seek("end")
> Sets the current byte position in file *file* to the end of *file* and returns that position.

file:setvbuf("no")
file:setvbuf("full"[, *size*])
file:setvbuf("line"[, *size*])
> Turns off buffering in file *file* such that writes occur immediately, turns on buffering such that *file*:flush() is required for writing, or turns on buffering such that only full lines are written at a time. Integer *size* specifies the maximum byte length of the buffer, and its default value is platform-specific.

> The default buffering for files is line buffering.

file:write(…)
> Writes the string or number argument values given to file *file* and returns *file* or, if an error occurred, returns nil followed by the error message.

---

file:flush()
> Saves any unwritten, buffered data to file *file*.

file:lines([...])   **Lua 5.2, 5.3, 5.4**
file:lines()   **Lua 5.1**
> Returns an iterator that can be used in a for loop to iter-
> ate over all lines in file *file*. Each line is read according
> to the formats specified by the argument values given,
> and the resulting values are assigned to loop variables.
> Table 9 lists the available formats. If no formats are spec-
> ified, "l" is used in Lua 5.3 and 5.4, while "*l" is used in
> Lua 5.1 and 5.2.

NOTE

The returned iterator does not automatically close *file*
when it is finished, as io.lines() does.

---

file:close()
> Closes file *file*, saving any unwritten, buffered data to it.
>
> In Lua 5.4, if *file* is a to-be-closed variable (i.e. it is a lo-
> cal variable with the attribute <close>), this will automati-
> cally be called when *file* goes out of scope. In Lua 5.1,
> 5.2, and 5.3, this will automatically be called when *file*
> is garbage-collected, though it could take a while.

io.type(*file*)
> Returns "file" if value *file* is an open file handle,
> "closed file" if *file* is a closed file handle, or nil if *file*
> is not a file handle.

Manage Files

Lua can manage files on a basic level. (The third-party module LuaFileSystem[9] provides a more complete interface to the
machine's underlying filesystem.)

os.rename(*oldname, newname*)
> Renames the file or directory identified by string *oldname*
> to string *newname* and returns true or, if an error occurred,
> returns nil followed by the error message and error
> code.

9   *http://keplerproject.github.io/luafilesystem/*

```
os.remove(filename)
```
Deletes the file or empty directory identified by string *filename* and returns **true** or, if an error occurred, returns **nil** followed by the error message and error code.

Start and Interact with a Process

Lua can start a process and read or write to it (but not both). Example 21 utilizes the underlying operating system as a way to obtain a directory's contents.

Example 21. Fetch the contents of a directory

```
local filenames = {}
local ls_command = "ls -1 " -- or "dir /B "
local p <close> = io.popen(ls_command .. dir)
for filename in p:lines() do
  filenames[#filenames + 1] = filename
end
```

```
io.popen(command[, mode])
```
Runs string shell command *command* in a separate process and returns a file handle for reading or writing to that process, depending on string *mode* (either "r" for read or "w" for write, not both). The default value for *mode* is "r".

In Lua 5.2, 5.3, and 5.4, when *file*:close() is called on the returned file handle, the values returned follow the same format as the values returned by os.execute().

Operating System Facilities

Lua's operating system module, **os**, contains tools for retrieving environment variables, executing shell commands, working with dates and times, and changing locale settings.

```
os.getenv(name)
```
Returns the string value of the environment variable whose name is string *name*, or **nil** if the variable is undefined.

```
os.execute(command)
```
Executes string shell command *command* and returns **true** if the command terminated successfully, followed by ei-

ther "exit" and an exit code if *command* terminated normally, or "signal" and a signal number if *command* was terminated by a signal. In Lua 5.1, returns the exit status of *command* only.

os.exit([*code*[, *close*]])   **Lua 5.2, 5.3, 5.4**
os.exit([*code*])   **Lua 5.1**
Terminates the current program with exit status *code*. In Lua 5.2, 5.3, and 5.4, *code* may be true (indicating normal exit), false (indicating abnormal exit), or a number. In Lua 5.1, *code* must be a number. The default value of *code* is true in Lua 5.2, 5.3, and 5.4, and 0 in Lua 5.1. If *close* is true, closes (if applicable in Lua 5.4), destroys, garbage-collects, and frees the memory used by all Lua values before terminating. This is useful when there are outstanding userdata created by the host that need to be destroyed properly. The default value of *close* is false.

Dates and Times

Lua can work with dates and times. Tables 10 and 11 list the date and time fields used by Lua's date and time facilities. Example 22 illustrates how to easily compute a future date from the current date.

Example 22. Compute a date 90 days in the future

```
local time = os.date("*t") -- e.g. 01 May 2017
time.day = time.day + 90
local future = os.time(time)
os.date("%d %b %Y", future) -- e.g. 30 Jul 2017
```

Table 10. Date and time table fields

Field	Description	Field	Description
year	Full year[a]	sec	Seconds of minute
month	Decimal month[a]	wday	1-based digit day of week
day	Decimal day[a]	yday	Decimal day of year
hour	24-hour hour (the default is 12)	isdst	Daylight savings time boolean

Field	Description	Field	Description
min	Minutes of hour		

Table 11. Date and time format fields

Field	Meaning	Field	Meaning
%a	Short day name	%p	AM or PM
%A	Full day name	%r	12-hour time of day
%b or %h	Short month name	%R	`%H:%M`
%B	Full month name	%S	Seconds of minute
%c	Locale-specific date and time	%T	`%H:%M:%S`
%C	Decimal century	%w	0-based digit day of week
%d	Decimal day	%W	Week of year
%D	`%m/%d/%y`	%x	Locale-specific date
%F	`%Y-%m-%d`	%X	Locale-specific time
%H	24-hour hour	%y	Short year
%I	12-hour hour	%Y	Full year
%j	Decimal day of year	%z	GMT-offset
%m	Decimal month of year	%Z	Time zone
%M	Minutes of hour	%%	Literal '%'

`os.time([t])`

Returns the time represented by table *t* or the current time. Table 10 lists the significant fields in *t* used to represent a date and time.

The time returned is the number of seconds elapsed since 01 January 1970, 00:00 UTC ("the epoch").

`os.difftime(time2, time1)`

Returns the difference in seconds between times *time2* and *time1*.

TIP

If sub-second precision is needed (e.g. when benchmarking a chunk of CPU-intensive Lua code), the difference between the values returned by successive calls to the function `os.clock()` should be sufficient.

---

os.date([*format*[, *time*]])
    Returns a formatted string representation of time *time* or the current time, subject to string *format*. *format* specifies the date and time fields to be included in the formatted string, and its default value is `"%c"`. Table 11 lists the available fields that *format* can have.

    If *format* starts with '!', *time* is formatted in Coordinated Universal Time (UTC).

os.date("*t"[, *time*])
os.date("!*t"[, *time*])
    Returns a table representation of time *time* or the current time, with the fields listed in Table 10. The prefix '!' indicates that the fields of the returned table should be in Coordinated Universal Time (UTC).

Locale Settings

Lua can alter the running program's current locale settings, which specify things like character classes (which characters belong to which class), how numbers and monetary balances are formatted, and how dates and times are displayed. Table 12 lists the locale categories that can be changed.

Table 12. Locale categories

Category	Description
`"all"`	Affects all categories.
`"collate"`	Affects string comparisons.
`"ctype"`	Affects string.lower(), string.upper(), and character classes in patterns.
`"monetary"`	Affects monetary formatting in C.
`"numeric"`	Affects number-to-string and string-to-number conversions.

Category	Description
`"time"`	Affects date and time fields in os.date().

```
os.setlocale(nil[, category])
os.setlocale(locale[, category])
```
Returns the current locale setting for string *category*, or changes the locale setting for *category* to *locale* (or the system's native locale if *locale* is "") and returns the new locale, or `nil` if the setting could not be changed. The set of available locales is system-dependent. *category* can be any of the categories listed in Table 12, and its default value is `"all"`.

Memory Management

Lua employs a garbage collector to manage memory by automatically deleting values no longer in use and freeing up the memory associated with them. While more often than not this is sufficient, Lua provides access controls for its collector should the need arise. For example, games may want to temporarily disable garbage collection at times when low latency is crucial.

```
collectgarbage(["collect"])
```
Performs a full garbage collection cycle.

```
collectgarbage("stop")
collectgarbage("restart")
```
Stops and restarts automatic garbage collection.

```
collectgarbage("isrunning")
```
Returns whether or not automatic garbage collection is on.

```
collectgarbage("count") * 1024
```
Returns the number of bytes of memory in use by Lua.

Miscellaneous

Lua provides other miscellaneous facilities.

arg
> List of command line arguments passed to the stand-
> alone Lua interpreter. Arguments passed to the Lua script
> being run start at index `1`. The name of the Lua script is
> at index `0`. Any arguments passed to the Lua interpreter,
> including the interpreter itself, have negative indices.
>
> This list will not exist in C programs that embed Lua un-
> less they explicitly define it.

print(…)
> Prints to `io.stdout` the string representation of all argu-
> ment values given, separated by tab characters ('\t').
>
> When it comes to determining a value's string represen-
> tation, Lua 5.4 relies on the metamethod `__tostring()`,
> while Lua 5.1, 5.2, and 5.3 rely on the function `to`
> `string()`.

_VERSION
> The Lua version string.

II

The Lua C API

C API Introduction

Lua itself is just a C library. Its three header files provide the host application with a simple API for creating an embedded Lua interpreter, interacting with it, and then closing it. Example 23 demonstrates a very basic stand-alone Lua interpreter whose command line accepts only a Lua script to run.

NOTE

The C examples in this book make use of some C99-specific features, so adapting those examples on a platform without a C99-compliant compiler will likely be necessary. However, Lua itself is written in ISO (ANSI) C, and will compile without modification.

Example 23. Simple stand-alone Lua interpreter

```
#include "lua.h"
#include "lauxlib.h"
#include "lualib.h"

int main(int argc, char **argv) {
  int status = 0;
  // Create a new embedded Lua interpreter.
  lua_State *L = luaL_newstate();
  // Load all of Lua's standard library modules.
  luaL_openlibs(L);
  // Execute the Lua script specified on the command
  // line. If there is an error, report it.
  if (argc > 1 && luaL_dofile(L, argv[1]) != LUA_OK†) {
    const char *errmsg = lua_tostring(L, -1);
    fprintf(stderr, "Lua error: %s\n", errmsg);
    status = 1;
  }
  // Close the Lua interpreter.
  lua_close(L);
  return status;
}
```

The header file *lua.h* provides Lua's basic C API. All functions and macros in that file start with the prefix "lua_". The file *lauxlib.h* provides a higher-level API with convenience func-

---

† LUA_OK does not exist in Lua 5.1, which uses the constant 0 instead.

tions for common tasks that involve the basic API. All functions and macros in that file start with the prefix "luaL_". The file *lualib.h* provides Lua's standard library module API. Table 13 lists the contents of *lualib.h* for hosts that prefer to load only specific Lua standard library modules rather than all of them at once.

This book refers to Lua's API functions and macros as "API functions" for the sake of simplicity.

CAUTION

Programming with Lua in C does not make programming in C any easier. Type-checking is mandatory, memory allocation errors are possible, and segmentation faults are nearly a given when passing improper arguments to Lua's API functions. Also, any unexpected errors raised by Lua will likely cause the host program to abort. (The section "Error and Warning Handling" on page 129 describes how to avoid that unhappy scenario.)

Table 13. Standard library module API (lualib.h)

Standard Library Module Name	C Function
""	luaopen_base
LUA_BITLIBNAME ("bit32")[a]	luaopen_bit32[a]
LUA_LOADLIBNAME ("package")	luaopen_package
LUA_MATHLIBNAME ("math")	luaopen_math
LUA_STRLIBNAME ("string")	luaopen_string
LUA_UTF8LIBNAME ("utf8")[b]	luaopen_utf8[b]
LUA_TABLIBNAME ("table")	luaopen_table
LUA_COLIBNAME ("coroutine")	luaopen_coroutine[c]
LUA_IOLIBNAME ("io")	luaopen_io
LUA_OSLIBNAME ("os")	luaopen_os
LUA_DBLIBNAME ("debug")	luaopen_debug

[a] Only in Lua 5.2.

[b] Not in Lua 5.1 or 5.2.

[c] Not in Lua 5.1, whose coroutine library module is included in luaopen_base.

lua_State
A C **struct** that represents both a thread in a Lua interpreter and the interpreter itself. Data can be shared between Lua threads but not between Lua interpreters.

TIP

Lua is fully re-entrant and can be used in multi-threaded code provided the macros **lua_lock** and **lua_unlock** are defined when compiling Lua.

---

lua_State *luaL_newstate();
Returns a newly created Lua interpreter, which is also that interpreter's main thread.

void luaL_openlibs(lua_State *L);
Loads all of Lua's standard library modules into Lua interpreter L.

luaL_requiref(L, *name*, *f*, 1), lua_pop(L, 1);   **Lua 5.2, 5.3, 5.4**
lua_pushcfunction(L, *f*), lua_pushstring(L, *name*),
                        lua_call(L, 1, 0);   **Lua 5.1**
Loads one of Lua's standard library modules into Lua interpreter L. *name* is the string name of the module to load and *f* is that module's C function. Table 13 lists Lua's standard library module names and their associated C functions.

Using this in place of luaL_openlibs() is useful for hosts that want control over which of Lua's standard library modules are available. For example, a host can prevent Lua code from interacting with the underlying operating system via the **os** module by simply not loading that module.

void lua_close(lua_State *L);
Destroys, garbage-collects, and frees the memory used by all values in Lua interpreter L. In Lua 5.4, also closes any to-be-closed variables.

Compiling Lua Programs

While a comprehensive guide to compiling Lua programs is beyond the scope of this book, the general idea is to provide a C compiler with the path to Lua's include files, and either compile Lua's *liblua.a* library directly into an executable, or dynamically link to a Lua shared library (e.g. *liblua5.4.so* or *lua54.dll*) if the platform supports it. For example, compiling Example 23 on page 87 using the GNU Compiler Collection (GCC) on Linux might look like:

```
# Compiling and linking to Lua shared library.
gcc -I /usr/include/lua5.4 -o ex23 ex23.c -llua5.4

# Compiling with Lua library directly.
gcc -I /path/to/lua5.4/include -o ex23 ex23.c \
    /path/to/lua5.4/liblua.a -lm -ldl
```

Note that paths and library names can vary from system to system depending on how and where Lua is installed.

The Stack

The primary method of communication between Lua and its host is through Lua's *stack*, which is treated as a "Last In, First Out" (LIFO) type of data structure. (The host however has complete access to all elements on Lua's stack and can manipulate them at will.) This book uses the term "the stack" to refer to the current Lua interpreter's stack. Communication between the host and Lua typically proceeds as follows:

1. The host pushes some C values onto the stack as Lua values.

2. The host invokes Lua to perform an operation on those values, such as defining a global variable, calling a function with arguments, or manipulating a table's contents. (During such an operation, Lua may call back into C via C functions, which are described in the section "C Functions" on page 114.)

3. The host retrieves any resulting Lua values from the stack as C values and then pops those Lua values off the stack or, if an error occurred, the host handles it gracefully.

Each element on the stack refers to a Lua value that was pushed onto it (either directly by the host or indirectly by Lua or its API functions during an operation). Also, each stack element has an *index*. Stack indices counting from the bottom of the stack are positive and start at 1, while stack indices counting from the top are negative and start at -1.

The stack has a finite size, so stack overflows are possible due to negligence. Ensuring that every value pushed onto the stack is eventually popped off helps maintain consistency. Where applicable, this book explicitly states how many stack values an API function pushes and pops.

The following sections describe how to prevent a stack overflow, how to work with stack indices, and how to push, pop, query, and retrieve stack values.

Increase Stack Size

Lua's initial stack size is 40 elements, though it is configurable when compiling Lua. The stack does not grow automatically as values are pushed onto it, so the host needs to grow it as necessary prior to pushing values in order to prevent a stack overflow.

`int lua_checkstack(lua_State *L, int n);`
Ensures the stack has room for pushing at least *n* more values onto it and returns 1 or, if the stack could not be grown any further, returns 0.

NOTE

The maximum stack size is 8,000 elements in Lua 5.1 and 15,000 elements in Lua 5.2, 5.3, and 5.4. This arbitrary limit is configurable when compiling Lua. It is possible to run out of memory before hitting the maximum stack size, especially in embedded environments.

Work with Stack Indices

The host can convert between relative and absolute stack indices, and retrieve or define the index of the stack top.

`int lua_absindex(lua_State *L, int index);`   **Lua 5.2, 5.3, 5.4**
Returns relative (negative) stack index *index* converted to an absolute (positive) index.

`int lua_gettop(lua_State *L);`
Returns the stack index of the value at the top of the

stack, which is also the number of values currently on the stack.

```
lua_settop(lua_State *L, int index);
```
> Makes the value at stack index *index* the value at the top of the stack, filling in any empty space with nil values and popping off any extra values. The stack has exactly `lua_absindex(L, index)` values on it after this operation.
>
> The stack size cannot be shrunk.

Push Values

The host can push various types of C values onto the stack as Lua values. The means for doing so are broken up into sections that cover how to push values of each of Lua's eight types: nil, boolean, number, string, function, table, thread, and userdata.

Push a nil

The host can push nil values onto the stack.

```
void lua_pushnil(lua_State *L);
```
> Pushes the value nil onto the stack.

Push a boolean

The host can push boolean values onto the stack.

```
void lua_pushboolean(lua_State *L, int b);
```
> Pushes boolean value *b* onto the stack.

Push a number

The host can push number values onto the stack. Lua provides some C type definitions that differentiate between integers and floats, since Lua numbers can be either.

```
lua_Integer
```
> The C type associated with Lua integers (typically `long long` in Lua 5.3 and 5.4, and `ptrdiff_t` in Lua 5.1 and 5.2). This is configurable when compiling Lua.

```
lua_Unsigned                                    Lua 5.2, 5.3, 5.4
```
The C type associated with unsigned Lua integers (typically unsigned long long in Lua 5.3 and 5.4, and unsigned long in Lua 5.2). This is configurable when compiling Lua.

```
lua_Number
```
The C type associated with Lua floats (typically double). This is configurable when compiling Lua.

```
void lua_pushinteger (lua_State *L, lua_Integer i);
void lua_pushunsigned(lua_State *L, lua_Unsigned i);   Lua 5.2
void lua_pushnumber  (lua_State *L, lua_Number n);
```
Pushes onto the stack integer value *i* or float value *n*.

Push a string

The host can push various kinds of string values onto the stack. Strings can be C-style strings, strings with embedded zeros, and formatted strings. Table 14 lists the placeholders available for formatted strings.

Table 14. String formatting placeholders

Placeholder	Argument Type	Meaning
%c	int	Character byte
%d	int	Integer
%f	lua_Number	Float
%I[a] (upper-case 'i')	lua_Integer	Integer
%p	Pointer	Hexadecimal address
%s	Zero-terminated string	String
%U[a]	long int	UTF-8 character
%%	N/A	Literal '%'

[a] Not in Lua 5.1 or 5.2.

```
const char *lua_pushstring  (lua_State *L,
                             const char *s);    Lua 5.2, 5.3, 5.4
void        lua_pushstring  (lua_State *L,
                             const char *s);          Lua 5.1
```

```
const char *lua_pushlstring (lua_State *L, const char *s,
                             size_t len);        Lua 5.2, 5.3, 5.4
void      lua_pushlstring (lua_State *L, const char *s,
                             size_t len);              Lua 5.1
const char *lua_pushliteral (lua_State *L,
                             "literal");         Lua 5.2, 5.3, 5.4
void      lua_pushliteral (lua_State *L, "literal"); Lua 5.1
const char *lua_pushfstring (lua_State *L,
                             const char *format, ...);
const char *lua_pushvfstring(lua_State *L,
                             const char *format,
                             va_list argp);
```

Pushes onto the stack zero-terminated string value *s*, string value *s* of length *len* bytes, a literal string value, formatted string value constructed from both string *for mat* and a variable number of arguments, or formatted string value constructed from both string *format* and variable argument list *argp*. Returns a pointer to Lua's internal copy of the string.

format contains a sequence of placeholders that specify how to format their respective arguments. Table 14 lists valid placeholders along with their meanings.

NOTE

Lua makes an internal copy of the given string. The host can immediately free that string after pushing it.

Push a string built from a buffer

The host can also push onto the stack a string value built from a string buffer. The process for pushing one of those strings is as follows:

1. Declare the buffer as a variable of type luaL_Buffer.
2. Initialize the buffer using luaL_buffinit() or luaL_buff initsize().
3. Fill the buffer using calls to luaL_addch(), luaL_addl string(), and luaL_addvalue(), or by filling in the string returned by luaL_buffinitsize().
4. Push the final string onto the stack using luaL_pushre sult() or luaL_pushresultsize().

While a buffer is in use, it utilizes a variable number of stack elements. Any non-buffer-related values that are pushed onto the stack should be popped prior to appending to the buffer.

Example 24 demonstrates how to push a string built from a string buffer whose final length is unknown ahead of time and Example 25 demonstrates how to push a string whose final length is known ahead of time.

Example 24. Push the entire contents of a file as a string

```
FILE *f = fopen(filename, "r");
luaL_Buffer b;
luaL_buffinit(L, &b);
char buf[BUFSIZ];
while (fgets(buf, BUFSIZ, f) != NULL)
  luaL_addlstring(&b, buf, strlen(buf));
luaL_pushresult(&b);
fclose(f);
```

Example 25. Push a lower-case copy of a string

```
luaL_Buffer b;
size_t len = strlen(s);
char *p = luaL_buffinitsize(L, &b, len);
for (int i = 0; i < len; i++)
  p[i] = tolower((unsigned char)s[i]);
luaL_pushresultsize(&b, len);
```

luaL_Buffer
  The C type associated with a Lua string buffer.

void luaL_buffinit(lua_State *L, luaL_Buffer *b);
  Initializes buffer *b*, a previously declared variable.

char *luaL_buffinitsize(lua_State *L, luaL_Buffer *b,
                        size_t *len*);   **Lua 5.2, 5.3, 5.4**
  Initializes buffer *b*, a previously declared variable, and returns a string of length *len* bytes that can be filled in and subsequently added to *b* using luaL_addsize().

```
void luaL_addchar    (luaL_Buffer *b, char ch);
void luaL_addlstring(luaL_Buffer *b, const char *s,
                     size_t len);
```
Adds to buffer *b* byte *ch* or string *s* of length *len* bytes.

```
const void luaL_addgsub(luaL_Buffer *b, const char *s,
                        const char *sub,
                        const char *repl);          Lua 5.4
```
Adds to buffer *b* a copy of string *s* with all instances of substring *sub* replaced with string *repl*.

```
void luaL_addvalue(luaL_Buffer *b);
```
Pops a value off the stack and adds its string representation to buffer *b*.

```
char *luaL_prepbuffer  (luaL_Buffer *b);
char *luaL_prepbuffsize(luaL_Buffer *b,
                        size_t size);          Lua 5.2, 5.3, 5.4
```
Returns a string of length LUAL_BUFFERSIZE or *size* bytes that can be filled in and subsequently added to buffer *b* using luaL_addsize().

```
void luaL_addsize(luaL_Buffer *b, size_t n);
```
Adds to buffer *b* *n* bytes from the string returned by luaL_buffinitsize(), luaL_prepbuffer() or luaL_prepbuff size().

```
void luaL_pushresult(luaL_Buffer *b);
```
Pushes onto the stack the value of buffer *b*.

```
void luaL_pushresultsize(luaL_Buffer *b,
                         size_t n);          Lua 5.2, 5.3, 5.4
```
Adds to buffer *b* *n* bytes from the string returned by luaL_buffinitsize(), luaL_prepbuffer() or luaL_prepbuff size(), and pushes onto the stack the resulting value of *b*.

Push a function

The host can push C function values onto the stack. However, not just any arbitrary C function can be pushed, but only those of type lua_CFunction that follow Lua's convention. The section "C Functions" on page 114 describes C functions in more detail.

Just as Lua functions can have upvalues (non-local, non-global variables), C functions can have them too. Upvalues in

C functions act just like C static variables and are available only in those functions. This is useful when functions need access to values that are neither arguments nor global variables. Example 29 on page 115 defines an upvalue to be the default value for a C function's table argument.

```
void lua_pushcfunction(lua_State *L, lua_CFunction f);
```
Pushes C function value *f* onto the stack.

```
void lua_pushcclosure(lua_State *L, lua_CFunction f,
                      int n);
```
Pops *n* values off the stack, associates them with C function *f* as upvalues, and pushes the resulting function (also called a *closure*) onto the stack.

f can use lua_upvalueindex(*i*) to fetch the stack index of upvalue number *i*, and through that index, retrieve the upvalue itself. The last value popped is the first upvalue (*i* = 1) and the first value popped is the last upvalue (*i* = *n*).

The maximum value for *n* is 256.

Push a table

The host can push only empty table values onto the stack (and fill them in later), since there is no C type for tables.

```
void lua_newtable   (lua_State *L);
void lua_createtable(lua_State *L, int nlist, int nhash);
```
Creates and pushes onto the stack a new, empty table with *nlist* pre-allocated list elements and *nhash* pre-allocated hash values.

List elements have integer keys from 1 to *nlist*, and hash values have keys of any other valid value.

TIP

lua_createtable() exists purely for performance reasons when table size and makeup are known ahead of time. All tables automatically grow in size as needed.

Push a thread

The host can push thread values onto the stack. The section "Threading in C" on page 133 covers how to work with thread values.

`lua_State *lua_newthread(lua_State *L);`
> Creates and pushes onto the stack a new (suspended) thread and returns a pointer to it. The new thread has its own stack, but shares the same global environment as Lua interpreter *L*.

`int lua_pushthread(lua_State *thread);`
> Pushes onto the stack thread *thread* and returns 1 if *thread* is the main thread (i.e. it was created with `luaL_newstate()`).

Push a userdata

The host can push onto the stack an instance of a C data type (typically a C `struct`) as a *full userdata* value. The host can also push onto the stack a regular C pointer as a *light userdata* value. Userdata values are treated like any other Lua value. By assigning a full userdata a metatable, that value can act like an object. (A light userdata cannot have a metatable.)

When pushing a full userdata onto the stack, Lua allocates a raw block of memory for it. The host is free to fill in and manipulate that block of memory as it sees fit. Since Lua itself cannot modify userdata values, the host is assured of data integrity. The host can also associate Lua values with full userdata. These *user values* are useful for keeping per-object Lua data, while maintaining a single metatable for similar objects. This concept is demonstrated in Example 8 on page 39. When Lua detects a full userdata is no longer in use, it frees the memory associated with it.

When pushing a light userdata onto the stack, Lua does not assume any responsibility for managing that value. The host is still obligated to do so.

Example 26 demonstrates how a C FILE* pointer can be used as a Lua value. Example 31 on page 125 provides a more complete picture of userdata by using C99's complex data types as Lua objects in a complex number module.

Example 26. Use a C structure as a Lua value

```
// C struct for using FILE* as a Lua value.
typedef struct {FILE *f;} File;

// Metamethod for closing to-be-closed files.
static int close_file(lua_State *L) {
  File *lf = (File *)luaL_checkudata(L, 1, "file_mt");
  lua_getiuservalue(L, 1, 1); // f closed?
  if (!lua_toboolean(L, -1)) {
    fclose(lf->f);
    lua_pushboolean(L, 1);
    lua_setiuservalue(L, 1, 1); // f closed now
  }
  return 0;
}

/* ... */

// Create a new file userdata, open and associate a
// file with it, assign a metatable that helps
// automatically close the file, and mark the userdata
// as a to-be-closed variable.
File *lf = lua_newuserdatauv(L, sizeof(File), 1);
lf->f = fopen(filename, "r");
lua_pushboolean(L, 0);
lua_setiuservalue(L, -2, 1); // f not closed yet
if (luaL_newmetatable(L, "file_mt")) {
  lua_pushcfunction(L, close_file);
  lua_setfield(L, -2, "__close");
}
```

```
lua_setmetatable(L, -2);
lua_toclose(L, -1);
/* do something with the file... */
lua_pop(L, 1); // invokes __close()
```

```
void *lua_newuserdatauv(lua_State *L, size_t size,
                        int nuvalues);                    Lua 5.4
void *lua_newuserdata  (lua_State *L, size_t size);
```
Allocates *size* bytes of memory, pushes it onto the stack as a userdata value, and returns a pointer to the allocated memory. The userdata can have *nuvalues* Lua values associated with it (only one in Lua 5.1, 5.2, and 5.3). The section "Miscellaneous" on page 143 describes how to associate these user values with userdata.

TIP

If a userdata does not need Lua values to be associated with it, the expression "`lua_newuserdatauv(L, size, 0)`" is more memory-efficient than "`lua_newuserdata(L, size)`".

```
void lua_pushlightuserdata(lua_State *L, void *p);
```
Pushes light userdata value *p* onto the stack.

Push an arbitrary value

The host can push onto the stack another reference to a value already on the stack.

```
void lua_pushvalue(lua_State *L, int index);
```
Pushes onto the stack another reference to the value at stack index *index*.

Add attributes to a pushed value

In Lua 5.4, the host can indicate that a value should be closed when it is popped from the stack. The section "Closing Metamethod" on page 35 describes how to define closing behavior.

```
void lua_toclose(lua_State *L, int index);               Lua 5.4
```
Indicates that the value at stack index *index* should have its metamethod __close() called when it is popped from the stack (e.g. when the current function returns to Lua, when there is an error, or when manually popped).

Only one value on the stack at a time can be marked in this way, and the host should only manually remove this value from the stack using lua_settop() or lua_pop().

Pop Values

The host can explicitly pop values off the stack. Even though some Lua API functions pop certain values off the stack, the host should not rely on Lua to manage the stack properly. All values pushed must eventually be popped in order to prevent a stack overflow.

NOTE

Once a value is popped off the stack, if it has no more references to it (i.e. it is no longer in use), Lua will delete that value and free the memory associated with it. Temporarily storing values in Lua's registry table is one way to prevent this from happening. The section "Reference Operations" on page 113 describes Lua's reference system.

---

void lua_pop(lua_State *L, int n);
    Pops n values off the stack.

void lua_remove(lua_State *L, int index);
    Removes the value at stack index index, shifting stack values above it towards the bottom of the stack.

Query Values

The host can query the stack for what types of values are at particular stack indices.

int lua_isnone   (lua_State *L, int index);
int lua_isnoneornil(lua_State *L, int index);
    Returns 1 if there is no value at stack index index or if that value is nil. Otherwise, returns 0.

int lua_isnil   (lua_State *L, int index);
int lua_isboolean   (lua_State *L, int index);
int lua_isinteger   (lua_State *L, int index);   **Lua 5.3, 5.4**
int lua_isnumber   (lua_State *L, int index);

```
int lua_isstring        (lua_State *L, int index);
int lua_istable         (lua_State *L, int index);
int lua_isfunction      (lua_State *L, int index);
int lua_iscfunction     (lua_State *L, int index);
int lua_isthread        (lua_State *L, int index);
int lua_isuserdata      (lua_State *L, int index);
int lua_islightuserdata(lua_State *L, int index);
```
Returns 1 if the value at stack index *index* is a nil, bool-
ean, integer, number (either an integer or a float), string,
table, function (either Lua or C), C function, thread, userdata (either full or light), or light userdata value. Otherwise, returns 0.

lua_isnumber() and lua_isstring() will return 1 if the
value is convertible to a number or string, respectively.
lua_type() may be more applicable in those cases.

```
int lua_type(lua_State *L, int index);
```
Returns the type of value at stack index *index*: LUA_TNONE
for a non-existent value, LUA_TNIL for nil, LUA_TBOOLEAN
for a boolean, LUA_TNUMBER for an integer or float, LUA_T
STRING for a string, LUA_TTABLE for a table, LUA_TFUNCTION
for a function, LUA_TTHREAD for a thread, LUA_TUSERDATA for
a userdata, or LUA_TLIGHTUSERDATA for a light userdata.

```
const char *lua_typename(lua_State *L, int type);
```
Returns the string name of value type *type*, which must
be one of the values returned by lua_type().

```
const char *luaL_typename(lua_State *L, int index);
```
Returns the string name of the type of value at stack index *index*.

Retrieve Values

The host can retrieve Lua values that are on the stack, converted to C values. The means for doing so are broken up
into sections that cover how to retrieve boolean, number,
string, function, thread, and userdata values. (Nil and table
values cannot be converted to C values.)

Retrieve a boolean

The host can retrieve boolean values that are on the stack, as
well as retrieve other types of stack values converted to bool-

eans.

```
int lua_toboolean(lua_State *L, int index);
```
Returns the value at stack index *index* converted to a boolean, where any value other than `false` and `nil` is considered boolean true.

Retrieve a number

The host can retrieve number values that are on the stack. Lua provides some C type definitions that differentiate between integers and floats, since Lua numbers can be either.

`lua_Integer`
The C type associated with Lua integers (typically `long long` in Lua 5.3 and 5.4, and `ptrdiff_t` in Lua 5.1 and 5.2). This is configurable when compiling Lua.

`lua_Unsigned`   **Lua 5.2, 5.3, 5.4**
The C type associated with unsigned Lua integers (typically `unsigned long long` in Lua 5.3 and 5.4, and `unsigned long` in Lua 5.2). This is configurable when compiling Lua.

`lua_Number`
The C type associated with Lua floats (typically `double`). This is configurable when compiling Lua.

```
lua_Integer  lua_tointeger  (lua_State *L, int index);
lua_Integer  lua_tointegerx (lua_State *L, int index,
                             int *isnum);            Lua 5.2, 5.3, 5.4
lua_Unsigned lua_tounsigned (lua_State *L, int index); Lua 5.2
lua_Unsigned lua_tounsignedx(lua_State *L, int index,
                             int *isnum);            Lua 5.2
lua_Number   lua_tonumber   (lua_State *L, int index);
lua_Number   lua_tonumberx  (lua_State *L, int index,
                             int *isnum);            Lua 5.2, 5.3, 5.4
```
Returns the value at stack index *index* converted to an integer or float, and sets *isnum* to `1` or, if the conversion fails, returns `0` and sets *isnum* to `0`.

Retrieve a string

The host can retrieve string values that are on the stack.

```
const char *lua_tostring  (lua_State *L, int index);
const char *lua_tolstring (lua_State *L, int index,
                               size_t *len);
const char *luaL_tolstring(lua_State *L, int index,
                               size_t *len);          Lua 5.2, 5.3, 5.4
```
Returns the value at stack index *index* converted to a C-style string and sets *len* to the byte length of the returned string or, if the conversion fails, returns NULL.

If the value has the metamethod __tostring(), luaL_tol string() calls that metamethod and returns the resulting string value instead. The section "Function Metamethods" on page 37 covers this metamethod in its generic form.

Retrieve a function

The host can retrieve C function values (not Lua function values) that are on the stack.

```
lua_CFunction lua_tocfunction(lua_State *L, int index);
```
Returns the value at stack index *index* converted to a C function or, if the conversion fails, returns NULL.

Retrieve a thread

The host can retrieve thread values that are on the stack.

```
lua_State *lua_tothread(lua_State *L, int index);
```
Returns the value at stack index *index* converted to a thread or, if the conversion fails, returns NULL.

Retrieve a userdata

The host can retrieve userdata values that are on the stack, regardless of whether they are full userdata or light userdata.

void *lua_touserdata(lua_State *L, int *index*);
Returns the value at stack index *index* converted to a userdata or, if the conversion fails, returns NULL.

Retrieve an arbitrary value

The host can retrieve the raw C pointer for a table, function, thread, or userdata value that is on the stack. However, this pointer has little practical use and is guaranteed to be valid only for as long as that value remains on the stack.

const void *lua_topointer(lua_State *L, int *index*);
Returns the string (Lua 5.4 only), function, table, thread, or userdata value at stack index *index* converted to a raw C pointer.

This is typically used only for hashing or debugging, as there is no way to retrieve the Lua value associated with a raw pointer.

Basic Stack Operations

The host can perform many different operations on stack values, such as element, global variable, arithmetic, relational, bitwise, string, length, and reference operations. The following sections cover these operations.

Element Operations

The host can perform simple stack element operations.

void lua_copy(lua_State *L, int *from*, int *to*);   **Lua 5.2, 5.3, 5.4**
Copies the value at stack index *from* to stack index *to*, overwriting the existing value.

void lua_insert(lua_State *L, int *index*);
Moves the value at the top of the stack to stack index *index*, shifting prior stack values towards the top of the stack.

```
void lua_replace(lua_State *L, int index);
```
Pops a value off the stack and moves it to stack index *index*, overwriting the existing value.

```
void lua_rotate(lua_State *L, int index, int n);    Lua 5.3, 5.4
```
Rotates the stack values between stack index *index* and the top of the stack (inclusive) by *n* positions towards the top of the stack. *n* can be negative.

Global Variable Operations

The host can define and retrieve global Lua variables.

```
void lua_setglobal(lua_State *L, const char *name);
```
Pops a value off the stack and assigns it to the global variable whose name is string *name*.

```
int  lua_getglobal(lua_State *L, const char *name); Lua 5.3, 5.4
void lua_getglobal(lua_State *L, const char *name); Lua 5.1, 5.2
```
Pushes onto the stack the value associated with the global variable whose name is string *name*, and returns the pushed value's type.

Arithmetic Operations

The host can invoke Lua's arithmetic operators. These operators may in turn invoke arithmetic metamethods, which are described in the section "Arithmetic Metamethods" on page 33.

```
void lua_arith(lua_State *L, LUA_OPADD);        Lua 5.2, 5.3, 5.4
void lua_arith(lua_State *L, LUA_OPSUB);        Lua 5.2, 5.3, 5.4
void lua_arith(lua_State *L, LUA_OPMUL);        Lua 5.2, 5.3, 5.4
void lua_arith(lua_State *L, LUA_OPDIV);        Lua 5.2, 5.3, 5.4
void lua_arith(lua_State *L, LUA_OPIDIV);           Lua 5.3, 5.4
void lua_arith(lua_State *L, LUA_OPMOD);        Lua 5.2, 5.3, 5.4
void lua_arith(lua_State *L, LUA_OPPOW);        Lua 5.2, 5.3, 5.4
```
Pops two values off the stack, adds (+), subtracts (-), multiplies (*), divides (/), integer divides (//), computes the remainder of floor division between (%), or exponentiates (∧) them, and pushes the resulting value onto the stack.

The first operand is the second value popped, and the

second operand is the first value popped.

void lua_arith(lua_State *L, LUA_OPUNM);   **Lua 5.2, 5.3, 5.4**
Pops a value off the stack, negates (-) it, and pushes the
resulting value onto the stack.

Relational Operations

The host can invoke Lua's relational operators. These operators may in turn invoke relational metamethods, which are
described in the section "Relational Metamethods" on page
33.

int lua_compare (lua_State *L, int *index1*, int *index2*,
               LUA_OPEQ);   **Lua 5.2, 5.3, 5.4**
int lua_equal   (lua_State *L, int *index1*,
               int *index2*);   **Lua 5.1**
int lua_compare (lua_State *L, int *index1*, int *index2*,
               LUA_OPLT);   **Lua 5.2, 5.3, 5.4**
int lua_lessthan(lua_State *L, int *index1*,
               int *index2*);   **Lua 5.1**
int lua_compare (lua_State *L, int *index1*, int *index2*,
               LUA_OPLE);   **Lua 5.2, 5.3, 5.4**
Compares the values at stack indices *index1* and *index2*
for equality (==), less than (<), or less than or equal to
(<=), and returns 1 if the comparison is correct or 0 if the
comparison is incorrect.

int lua_rawequal(lua_State *L, int *index1*, int *index2*);
Returns 1 if the values at stack indices *index1* and *index2*
are equal, bypassing all metamethods. Otherwise, returns
0.

Bitwise Operations

The host can invoke the bitwise operators introduced in Lua
5.3. These operators may in turn invoke bitwise metamethods, which are described in the section "Bitwise Metamethods" on page 34.

void lua_arith(lua_State *L, LUA_OPBAND);   **Lua 5.3, 5.4**
void lua_arith(lua_State *L, LUA_OPBOR);   **Lua 5.3, 5.4**
void lua_arith(lua_State *L, LUA_OPBXOR);   **Lua 5.3, 5.4**
Pops two values off the stack, performs bitwise AND

(&), OR (|), or XOR (~) on them, and pushes the resulting value onto the stack.

The first operand is the second value popped, and the second operand is the first value popped.

```
void lua_arith(lua_State *L, LUA_OPBNOT);          Lua 5.3, 5.4
```
Pops a value off the stack, performs bitwise NOT (~) on it, and pushes the resulting value onto the stack.

```
void lua_arith(lua_State *L, LUA_OPSHL);           Lua 5.3, 5.4
void lua_arith(lua_State *L, LUA_OPSHR);           Lua 5.3, 5.4
```
Pops two values off the stack, performs left shift (<<) or right shift (>>) on them, and pushes the resulting value onto the stack.

The first operand is the second value popped, and the second operand is the first value popped.

String Operations

The host can invoke Lua's string concatenation (..) and length (#) operators. These operators may in turn invoke their respective metamethods, which are covered in the section "Other Operator and Statement Metamethods" on page 35. The host can also take advantage of a convenience function for performing global substitution in strings.

```
void lua_concat(lua_State *L, int n);
```
Pops *n* values off the stack, concatenates them as strings, and pushes the resulting value onto the stack.

```
void lua_len(lua_State *L, int index);             Lua 5.2, 5.3, 5.4
```
Pushes onto the stack the length (#) of the value at stack index *index*.

```
lua_Integer luaL_len  (lua_State *L, int index);   Lua 5.3, 5.4
int         luaL_len  (lua_State *L, int index);   Lua 5.2
size_t      lua_objlen(lua_State *L, int index);   Lua 5.1
```
Returns the length (#) of the value at stack index *index*.

```
const char *luaL_gsub(lua_State *L, const char *s,
                const char *sub, const char *repl);
```
Pushes onto the stack a copy of string *s* with all instances of substring *sub* replaced with string *repl*, and returns the new string.

sub is not interpreted as a Lua pattern.

Table Operations

The host can interact with tables in many different ways. The following sections describe how to retrieve the value associated with a table key, how to assign a value to a table key, and how to iterate over a table's key-value pairs.

Retrieve the value assigned to a key

The host can retrieve values assigned to table keys. These operations may invoke the metafield __index or metamethod __index(), both of which are covered in the section "Other Operator and Statement Metamethods" on page 35.

```
int  lua_gettable(lua_State *L, int index);        Lua 5.3, 5.4
void lua_gettable(lua_State *L, int index);        Lua 5.1, 5.2
int  lua_rawget  (lua_State *L, int index);        Lua 5.3, 5.4
void lua_rawget  (lua_State *L, int index);        Lua 5.1, 5.2
```
Pops a key off the stack, pushes the value in the table at stack index *index* associated with that key, and returns the pushed value's type.

lua_rawget() bypasses all metamethods.

```
int  lua_geti   (lua_State *L, int index,
                 lua_Integer i);                   Lua 5.3, 5.4
int  lua_rawgeti(lua_State *L, int index,
                 lua_Integer i);                   Lua 5.3, 5.4
void lua_rawgeti(lua_State *L, int index, int i);  Lua 5.1, 5.2
```
Pushes onto the stack the ith element of the list at stack index *index*, and returns the pushed element's type.

lua_rawgeti() bypasses all metamethods.

```
int  lua_getfield(lua_State *L, int index,
                  const char *key);                Lua 5.3, 5.4
void lua_getfield(lua_State *L, int index,
                  const char *key);                Lua 5.1, 5.2
```
Pushes onto the stack the value associated with string *key* in the table at stack index *index*, and returns the pushed value's type.

```
int  lua_rawgetp(lua_State *L, int index,
                 const void *p);                        Lua 5.3, 5.4
void lua_rawgetp(lua_State *L, int index,
                 const void *p);                             Lua 5.2
```
Pushes onto the stack the value associated with light userdata *p* in the table at stack index *index* (bypassing all metamethods), and returns the pushed value's type.

```
int luaL_getsubtable(lua_State *L, int index,
                     const char *key);          Lua 5.2, 5.3, 5.4
```
Pushes onto the stack an existing or newly created table value assigned to string *key* in the table at stack index *index*, and returns 1 if the pushed table already existed or 0 if it was created.

Assign a value to a key

The host can fill in a table with key-value pairs. These operations may invoke the __newindex metafield or __newindex() metamethod, both of which are covered in the section "Other Operator and Statement Metamethods" on page 35.

```
void lua_settable(lua_State *L, int index);
void lua_rawset  (lua_State *L, int index);
```
Pops two values off the stack and associates them as a key-value pair in the table at stack index *index*.

The second value popped is the key and the first value popped is the value.

lua_rawset() bypasses all metamethods.

```
void lua_seti   (lua_State *L, int index,
                 lua_Integer i);                        Lua 5.3, 5.4
void lua_rawseti(lua_State *L, int index,
                 lua_Integer i);                        Lua 5.3, 5.4
void lua_rawseti(lua_State *L, int index, int i);   Lua 5.1, 5.2
```
Pops a value off the stack and makes it the ith element in the list at stack index *index*.

lua_rawseti() bypasses all metamethods.

```
void lua_setfield(lua_State *L, int index,
                  const char *key);
```
Pops a value off the stack and associates it with string *key* to make a key-value pair in the table at stack index

index.

```
void lua_rawsetp(lua_State *L, int index,
                 const void *p);
```
Lua 5.2, 5.3, 5.4

Pops a value off the stack and associates it with light userdata *p* to make a key-value pair in the table at stack index *index*, bypassing all metamethods.

TIP

Light userdata can be used as unique keys in Lua's registry table without having to appeal to Lua's reference system. The section "Reference Operations" on page 113 describes the registry.

Iterate over a table

The host can iterate over all key-value pairs in a table using the following procedure:

1. Push the table to be iterated over onto the stack.
2. Push the value `nil` using `lua_pushnil()`.
3. Continually call `lua_next()` while its return value is non-zero.
4. For each iteration, a key is just below the top of the stack and its associated value is at the top of the stack.
5. Before the next iteration, pop the value off the stack, leaving the current key.
6. If a new key-value pair was added during the iteration, pop the key as well and push `nil` in order to restart iteration from the beginning. (Any key-value pairs edited or deleted during iteration do not require a restart.)

Iteration order is not defined, even if the table is a list.

CAUTION

If a key is numeric, calling `lua_tostring()` or `lua_tol string()` on it will actually change that key into a string and adversely affect the next call to `lua_next()`.

Example 27 illustrates how to iterate over a table and delete all of its key-value pairs whose keys are strings.

Example 27. Delete all string keys from a table

```
/* push table to be iterated over... */
lua_pushnil(L);
while (lua_next(L, -2) != 0) {
  if (lua_type(L, -2) == LUA_TSTRING) {
    // Delete values assigned to string keys (fields).
    const char *key = lua_tostring(L, -2);
    lua_pushnil(L);
    lua_setfield(L, -4, key);
  }
  lua_pop(L, 1); // value
}
lua_pop(L, 1); // table iterated over
```

```
int lua_next(lua_State *L, int index);
```
Pops a key off the stack and pushes onto the stack the next key-value pair from the table at stack index *in dex*. If there are no more key-value pairs to push, returns 0.

The pushed value is at the top of the stack and the pushed key is just below it.

NOTE

Modifying a table during traversal is permitted as long as no new key-value pairs are added. If a new pair is added, traversal must begin anew.

Length Operations

The host can invoke Lua's length operator. This operator may in turn invoke the length metamethod, which is covered in the section "Other Operator and Statement Metamethods" on page 35.

```
void lua_len(lua_State *L, int index);          Lua 5.2, 5.3, 5.4
```
Pushes onto the stack the length (#) of the value at stack index *index*.

```
lua_Integer luaL_len(lua_State *L, int index);   Lua 5.3, 5.4
int         luaL_len(lua_State *L, int index);   Lua 5.2
```
Returns the length (#) of the value at stack index *index*.

```
lua_Unsigned lua_rawlen(lua_State *L, int index);      Lua 5.4
size_t       lua_rawlen(lua_State *L, int index);   Lua 5.2, 5.3
size_t       lua_objlen(lua_State *L, int index);      Lua 5.1
```
Returns the length of the string, table, or userdata value at stack index *index*, bypassing all metamethods.

Reference Operations

The stack is only meant for storing temporary values prior to performing a stack operation. (Once a value is popped from the stack, Lua may garbage-collect it.) When the host needs to store values for later use, it can either assign those values to global Lua variables (which may not be ideal), or use an internal *registry* table that Lua provides for storing and retrieving any Lua values. Lua's registry exists at the special stack index LUA_REGISTRYINDEX (which is not a true stack index, so it cannot be popped, removed, replaced, rotated, etc.). The registry is accessible only through Lua's C API, ensuring integrity.[10]

NOTE

By convention, string keys comprising an underscore followed by one or more upper-case letters are reserved for use by Lua itself in its registry.

Since the registry is also available to any external Lua C modules the host loads, there is a possibility of key clashes. In order to avoid this, Lua provides a way to store and retrieve unique references to Lua values in the registry (but does not require the host to utilize it). Example 32 on page 131 uses the registry to store and retrieve a sandboxed environment for running potentially unsafe code in.

CAUTION

When manually adding key-value pairs to Lua's registry, integer keys may not be used, as that will interfere with Lua's unique reference system.

---

10 Technically, Lua's standard library module debug can access the registry, but the host can choose not to load that module or to disable it.

```
int luaL_ref(lua_State *L, LUA_REGISTRYINDEX);
```
> Pops a value off the stack, creates a unique integer reference to it in Lua's registry table, and returns that reference.
>
> The referenced value will not be eligible for garbage collection at least until luaL_unref() is called for that value.

```
int lua_rawgeti(lua_State *L, LUA_REGISTRYINDEX, int ref);
```
> Pushes onto the stack the value associated with the unique integer reference *ref* returned by luaL_ref(), and returns the pushed value's type.

```
void luaL_unref(lua_State *L, LUA_REGISTRYINDEX, int ref);
```
> Releases integer reference *ref* to the value in Lua's registry table. That value may now be garbage-collected if it is no longer being used.

C Functions

A C function is a special kind of function that Lua can interact with. It is just like a normal C function, except it has a specific type:

```
typedef int (*lua_CFunction) (lua_State *L);
```

Functions of this type receive their arguments from the stack and push their return values onto the stack. C functions are a subset of Lua's first-class function values and behave in exactly the same way. The following sections describe how to define, register, and call C functions.

Define a C Function

C functions are defined using the type lua_CFunction and follow the form of a normal C function definition. When a C function is called, it receives its own stack, which contains only the argument values passed to that function (the first argument is at the bottom of the stack and the last argument is at the top of the stack). When the C function is finished, it should push its return values onto its stack (starting with the first return value) and then return the number of return values pushed. Example 28 defines and makes available a simple C function that returns the value of C99's gamma function for a given number argument.

Example 28. Mathematical gamma function

```
static int gamma(lua_State *L) {
  double z = luaL_checknumber(L, 1); // fetch argument
  lua_pushnumber(L, tgamma(z)); // push value to return
  return 1; // number of stack values to return
}

/* ... */

// Add gamma to Lua's math module.
lua_getglobal(L, "math");
lua_pushcfunction(L, gamma);
lua_setfield(L, -2, "gamma");
lua_pop(L, 1); // global "math"
```

A C function's stack is independent of the "main" stack and any other active C function stack. The function is not required to pop argument values off its stack, as the stack is discarded after the function returns. (The function is not even required to pop off any intermediate values it pushed, so long as there is enough stack space for its return values.)

Lua provides a number of convenient API functions designed specifically for C functions. These functions are broken up into sections that cover how to validate and retrieve argument values, how to retrieve upvalues, and how to prevent a stack overflow. (C functions are not limited to using these API functions, however.) Example 29 exhibits a few of these convenience functions and concepts.

Example 29. C function that translates string characters

```
static int translate_chars(lua_State *L) {
  // Fetch arguments. The first should be a string. The
  // second should be a table, if given. Otherwise, use
  // a default table stored as an upvalue.
  const char *s = luaL_checkstring(L, 1);
  if (lua_gettop(L) > 1)
    luaL_checktype(L, 2, LUA_TTABLE);
  else
    lua_pushvalue(L, lua_upvalueindex(1));
```

```
  // Allocate and fill a copy of the string argument,
  // translate its characters according to the table
  // argument, and push the result.
  char *o = strcpy(malloc(strlen(s) + 1), s);
  for (char *p = o; *p; p++) {
    lua_pushlstring(L, p, 1); // table key
    lua_gettable(L, 2); // fetch value assigned to key
    if (lua_isstring(L, -1))
      *p = *lua_tostring(L, -1); // translate char
    lua_pop(L, 2); // table key and value
  }
  lua_pushstring(L, o); // push the value to return
  free(o);
  return 1; // the number of stack values to return
}

/* ... */

// Create the default translation table, assign it as
// an upvalue to translate_chars, and register that
// function as the global function "tr".
lua_createtable(L, 0, 1);
lua_pushliteral(L, "_");
lua_setfield(L, -2, " "); // translate ' ' to '_'
lua_pushcclosure(L, translate_chars, 1);
lua_setglobal(L, "tr");

-- Lua code.
tr("hello world!") -- returns "hello_world!"
tr("hello!", {["!"] = "?"}) -- returns "hello?"
```

Validate and retrieve argument value types

The host can conveniently validate argument value types
while retrieving them converted to C values.

lua_Integer	luaL_checkinteger (lua_State *L, int arg);	
int	luaL_checkint (lua_State *L, int arg);	Lua 5.1, 5.2
long	luaL_checklong (lua_State *L, int arg);	Lua 5.1, 5.2
lua_Unsigned	luaL_checkunsigned(lua_State *L, int arg);	Lua 5.2
lua_Number	luaL_checknumber (lua_State *L, int arg);	
const char	*luaL_checkstring (lua_State *L, int arg);	

```
const char  *luaL_checklstring(lua_State *L, int arg,
                                size_t *len);
void        *luaL_checkudata  (lua_State *L, int arg,
                                const char *name);
```
Asserts that function argument number *arg* is an integer
value, number value (either an integer or a float), string
value, or userdata value whose metatable is the metatable identified by string *name*, and returns that value
converted to its respective C type, or raises an error.

luaL_checklstring() sets *len* to the byte length of the returned string.

```
void *luaL_testudata(lua_State *L, int arg,
                      const char *name);        Lua 5.2, 5.3, 5.4
```
Returns the value of function argument number *arg* con-
verted to a userdata, provided its metatable is the metatable identified by string *name*, or returns NULL if that
value is not the desired type of userdata.

```
void luaL_checktype(lua_State *L, int arg, int type);
```
Asserts that function argument number *arg* is Lua type
type, or raises an error.

```
const char *luaL_typeerror(lua_State *L, int arg,
                            const char *name);        Lua 5.4
int        luaL_typerror (lua_State *L, int arg,
                            const char *name);        Lua 5.1
```
Raises an error that function argument number *arg* is not
of string type *name*. *name* is typically the name of a custom
userdata type.

Validate argument values

The host can conveniently validate that argument values exist
or satisfy a condition.

```
void luaL_checkany(lua_State *L, int arg);
```
Asserts that function argument number *arg* was given, or
raises an error.

```
void luaL_argcheck(lua_State *L, int expr, int arg,
                    const char *message);
```
Asserts that expression *expr* evaluates to a non-zero
value, or raises an error that implicates function argument number *arg* with string *message* as additional error

information.

```
void luaL_argexpected(lua_State *L, int expr, int arg,
                      const char *name);              Lua 5.4
```
Asserts that expression *expr* evaluates to a non-zero value, or raises an error that function argument number *arg* is not of string type *name*.

```
void luaL_argerror(lua_State *L, int arg,
                   const char *message);
```
Raises an error that implicates function argument number *arg* with string *message* as additional error information.

Specify default argument values

The host can conveniently retrieve argument values converted to C values, or retrieve default values.

```
lua_Integer  luaL_optinteger (lua_State *L, int arg,
                              lua_Integer default);
int          luaL_optint     (lua_State *L, int arg,
                              int default);          Lua 5.1, 5.2
long         luaL_optlong     (lua_State *L, int arg,
                              long default);         Lua 5.1, 5.2
lua_Unsigned luaL_optunsigned(lua_State *L, int arg,
                              lua_Unsigned default);  Lua 5.2
lua_Number   luaL_optnumber  (lua_State *L, int arg,
                              lua_Number default);
const char  *luaL_optstring  (lua_State *L, int arg,
                              const char *default);
const char  *luaL_optlstring (lua_State *L, int arg,
                              const char *default,
                              size_t *len);
```
Returns the value of function argument number *arg* converted to an integer, float, or string, defaulting to *default* if the argument value does not exist or is nil, or, if the conversion fails, raises an error.

luaL_optlstring() sets *len* to the byte length of the returned string.

```
int luaL_checkoption(lua_State *L, int arg,
                     const char *default,
                     const char *const list[]);
```
Asserts that function argument number *arg* is a string included in NULL-terminated string list *list*, and returns the index of that string in *list*, or raises an error. If given,

the default value for argument number *arg* is string *de
fault*.

Retrieve upvalue indices

The host can retrieve the stack indices of a C function's upvalues.

```
int lua_upvalueindex(int i);
```
Returns the stack index of the ith upvalue of the current
function.

The returned index can be used in most API functions
involving stack indices, but since it is not a true stack index, it cannot be popped, removed, replaced, rotated,
etc.

Raise an error or emit a warning

The host can raise errors from within C functions. Raising an
error outside of a C function triggers Lua's panic function and
will most likely result in a hard abort. Lua 5.4 also allows the
host to emit warnings.

```
int luaL_error(lua_State *L, const char *format, ...);
```
Raises an error with a formatted error message constructed from string *format* and a variable number of arguments. *format* contains a sequence of placeholders
that specify how to format their respective arguments.
Table 14 on page 93 lists valid placeholders along with
their meanings.

If available, filename and line number information is automatically prepended to the error message.

```
int lua_error(lua_State *L);
```
Raises a Lua error whose error message is at the top of
the stack.

TIP

The statements "`return luaL_error(L, ...);`" and "`return
lua_error(L);`" are idioms in C functions, signaling that
the function immediately halts execution.

```
void lua_warning(lua_State *L, const char *message,
                 int tocontinue);                    Lua 5.4
```
Emits a warning with string *message*. *tocontinue* is a flag that indicates whether or not the warning message will continue in a subsequent call to this function.

Warnings are handled by the function given to lua_set warnf(), which by default prints warnings to standard error (stderr).

Increase stack size

A C function's initial stack size is $n + 20$ elements, where n is the number of argument values already on the stack when the function is called. (This default size is configurable when compiling Lua.) The stack does not grow automatically as values are pushed onto it, so the host needs to grow it as necessary prior to pushing values in order to prevent a stack overflow.

```
void luaL_checkstack(lua_State *L, int n, const char *msg);
```
Asserts that the stack can grow by *n* more values, or raises an error with error message string *msg*.

NOTE

The maximum stack size is 8,000 elements in Lua 5.1 and 15,000 elements in Lua 5.2, 5.3, and 5.4. This arbitrary limit is configurable when compiling Lua. It is possible to run out of memory before hitting the maximum stack size, especially in embedded environments.

Register a C Function

The host can conveniently assign a C function to a global variable. (C functions may also be assigned to table keys using various other API functions.)

```
void lua_register(lua_State *L, const char *name,
                  lua_CFunction f);
```
Assigns C function *f* to the global variable whose name is string *name*.

Call a C Function

The host can call a C function (or any Lua function for that matter) using the following procedure:

1. Push the function to call onto the stack.
2. Push onto the stack the argument values to pass to the function, starting with the first argument value.
3. Call the function using one of Lua's API functions.
4. Process any resulting values returned by the function and pop them off the stack. (The last value returned is at the top of the stack.)

Example 30 demonstrates how to call the Lua function str ing.find() and handle the variable number of values it returns (zero in the case of no match, two in the case of a match with no captures, and three or more in the case of a match with captures).

Example 30. Call Lua's string.find

```
// Record initial stack size due to LUA_MULTRET.
int n = lua_gettop(L);
// Push the global function string.find().
lua_getglobal(L, "string");
lua_getfield(L, -1, "find");
lua_replace(L, -2);
// Push two arguments.
lua_pushstring(L, s);
lua_pushstring(L, pattern);
// Call the function with those two arguments,
// expecting a variable number of results.
if (lua_pcall(L, 2, LUA_MULTRET, 0) == LUA_OK† &&
    lua_gettop(L) > n) {
  int start = lua_tointeger(L, n + 1);
  int end = lua_tointeger(L, n + 2);
  /* process returned positions and any captures... */
  lua_settop(L, n); // pop all returned values
}
```

```
void lua_call (lua_State *L, int nargs, int nresults);
int  lua_pcall(lua_State *L, int nargs, int nresults,
               int error_handler);
```
Pops *nargs* function argument values off the stack, pops

---

†   LUA_OK does not exist in Lua 5.1, which uses the constant 0 instead.

off the stack the function that is now at the top of the stack, calls that popped function with the popped arguments (the last value popped being the first argument and the first value popped being the last argument), and pushes the first *nresults* values returned by the function onto the stack (or all of them if *nresults* is LUA_MULTRET). lua_pcall() returns LUA_OK (or 0 in Lua 5.1) on success.

lua_call() should only be called from within C functions that do not care to handle errors and have been ultimately invoked by a protected call. The section "Error and Warning Handling" on page 129 describes protected calls.

If an error occurs, lua_pcall() pushes the error message onto the stack and returns a non-zero error code. If *error_handler* is nonzero, the function at stack index *error_handler* is called with the error message as an argument, and that function's return value is the error message ultimately pushed onto the stack. Table 15 on page 129 lists Lua's error codes and their meanings.

If the value being called is a table or userdata value with the metamethod __call(), that metamethod is called to perform the operation. The section "Other Operator and Statement Metamethods" on page 35 covers this metamethod in its generic form.

```
int lua_cpcall(lua_State *L, lua_CFunction f,
               void *userdata);                    Lua 5.1
```
Calls C function *f* with userdata *userdata* as that function's only argument value and returns 0 on success.

If an error occurs, the error message is pushed onto the stack and a non-zero error code is returned instead. Table 15 on page 129 lists Lua's error codes and their meanings.

Metatables

The host can create metatables, assign and retrieve the metatables of values, call specific metamethods, and retrieve specific metafields. The means for doing so are described in the following sections. The section "Metatables and Metamethods" on page 32 describes metatables, metamethods, and meta-fields.

Create or Fetch a Metatable

The host can specifically create a metatable, as opposed to creating a generic table and using it as a metatable. The host can also easily fetch a previously created metatable by name.

int luaL_newmetatable(lua_State *L, const char *name);
Pushes onto the stack the metatable identified by string *name*, and returns 1 if the metatable had to be created first or 0 if the metatable already existed.

CAUTION

Lua keeps track of all metatable names in the same place. If the host loads any external C modules, those modules will also have the ability to create their own metatables, so there is a possibility of name clashes.

Assign a Metatable

The host can assign a metatable to a value (bypassing the metafield __metatable that value may have). In the C API, values are not limited to tables and userdata, but can be any Lua value. However, only tables and userdata can have individual metatables. All other types each share a single metatable.

int lua_setmetatable(lua_State *L, int *index*);   **Lua 5.1, 5.4**
void lua_setmetatable(lua_State *L, int *index*);   **Lua 5.2, 5.3**
Pops a table value off the stack and assigns it to be the metatable of the value at stack index *index*. Always returns 1 in Lua 5.1 and 5.4.

void luaL_setmetatable(lua_State *L,
                       const char *name);   **Lua 5.2, 5.3, 5.4**
Assigns the metatable identified by string *name* to be the metatable of the value at the top of the stack.

Retrieve a Metatable

The host can retrieve a value's metatable.

```
int lua_getmetatable(lua_State *L, int index);
```
Pushes onto the stack the metatable associated with the value at stack index *index* and returns 1, or, if that value has no metatable, pushes nothing and returns 0.

```
int luaL_getmetatable(lua_State *L,
                  const char *name);          Lua 5.3, 5.4
void luaL_getmetatable(lua_State *L,
                  const char *name);          Lua 5.1, 5.2
```
Pushes onto the stack the metatable identified by string *name* or nil if no metatable was found, and returns the pushed value's type.

Metamethods and Metafields

The host can call specific metamethods and retrieve specific metafields.

```
int luaL_callmeta(lua_State *L, int index,
                  const char *name);
```
Calls the metamethod named string *name* that belongs to the metatable associated with the value at stack index *index*, pushes onto the stack the value returned by that call, and returns 1. If the metamethod does not exist, returns 0 and pushes nothing. The metamethod is passed the stack value as its only argument.

```
int luaL_getmetafield(lua_State *L, int index,
                  const char *key);
```
Pushes onto the stack the value associated with string *key* in the metatable associated with the value at stack index *index*, and returns the pushed value's type. If the metafield does not exist, returns LUA_TNIL and pushes nothing.

C Modules

Lua provides an API for creating loadable C modules, which are typically just Lua tables. A C module often contains:

- A set of Lua C functions specific to the module.
- An array of type `luaL_Reg[]` that maps those C functions to string names in the module's table.
- A Lua C function that serves as the module's entry point. This function creates the module table and pushes it onto the stack as a return value. By convention, the function's name is "`luaopen_name`," where *name* is the module's actual name (the string that would be passed to Lua's `require()` function). Any '.' characters in *name* should be replaced with '_' and any "*-version*" suffix should be ignored. For example, a module named "lpeg" has the entry point "`luaopen_lpeg`", a submodule named "utf8.ext" has the entry point "`luaopen_utf8_ext`", and a versioned submodule named "utf8.ext-v2" has the same entry point "`luaopen_utf8_ext`".

Example 31 lists a module that provides an interface to C99's complex numbers.

Example 31. Complex number module

```
#include <complex.h>
#include "lua.h"
#include "lauxlib.h"

typedef double complex Complex;

// Pushes a complex number as userdata.
static int pushcomplex(lua_State *L, Complex z) {
  Complex *p = lua_newuserdatauv(L, sizeof(Complex),
                                 0);
  *p = z;
  luaL_setmetatable(L, "complex_mt");
  return 1;
}

// Creates and pushes a new complex number.
static int complex_new(lua_State *L) {
  double x = luaL_optnumber(L, 1, 0);
  double y = luaL_optnumber(L, 2, 0);
  pushcomplex(L, x + y * I);
  return 1;
}
```

```
// Asserts and returns a complex number function
// argument.
static Complex checkcomplex(lua_State *L, int arg) {
  return lua_isuserdata(L, 1) ?
    *((Complex *)luaL_checkudata(L, arg, "complex_mt"))
    : luaL_checknumber(L, arg);
}

// Defines a unary complex number operation.
#define unop(name, op) \
  static int complex_##name(lua_State *L) { \
    Complex z = checkcomplex(L, 1); \
    return pushcomplex(L, op(z)); \
  }

// Defines a binary complex number operation.
#define binop(name, op) \
  static int complex_##name(lua_State *L) { \
    Complex z1 = checkcomplex(L, 1); \
    Complex z2 = checkcomplex(L, 2); \
    return pushcomplex(L, z1 op z2); \
  }

// Complex number operations.
unop(abs, cabs)
unop(real, creal)
unop(imag, cimag)
unop(arg, carg)
unop(conj, conj)
binop(add, +)
binop(sub, -)
binop(mul, *)
binop(div, /)
unop(unm, -)
binop(eq, ==)

// String representation of a complex number.
static int complex_tostring(lua_State *L) {
  Complex z = checkcomplex(L, 1);
  double x = creal(z), y = cimag(z);
  if (x != 0 && y > 0)
    lua_pushfstring(L, "%f+%fi", x, y);
  else if (x != 0 && y < 0)
    lua_pushfstring(L, "%f%fi", x, y);
  else if (x == 0)
    lua_pushfstring(L, "%fi", y);
```

```
  else
    lua_pushfstring(L, "%f", x);
  return 1;
}

// Complex module functions.
static const luaL_Reg complex_functions[] = {
  {"new", complex_new},
  {"abs", complex_abs},
  {"real", complex_real},
  {"imag", complex_imag},
  {"arg", complex_arg},
  {"conj", compex_conj},
  {NULL, NULL}
};

// Complex number metamethods.
static const luaL_Reg complex_metamethods[] = {
  {"__add", complex_add},
  {"__sub", complex_sub},
  {"__mul", complex_mul},
  {"__div", complex_div},
  {"__unm", complex_unm},
  {"__eq", complex_eq},
  {"__tostring", complex_tostring},
  {NULL, NULL}
};

// Complex number module entry point.
int luaopen_complex(lua_State *L) {
  // Create and push the module table.
  luaL_newlib(L, complex_functions);
  // Create the complex number metatable, fill it,
  // link it with the module table, then pop it.
  luaL_newmetatable(L, "complex_mt");
  luaL_setfuncs(L, complex_metamethods, 0);
  lua_pushvalue(L, -2); // the module table
  lua_setfield(L, -2, "__index");
  lua_pop(L, 1); // metatable
  return 1; // return the module table
}

-- Lua code.
local complex = require("complex")
complex.new(3, 4) + complex(-1, -2) -- results in 2+2i
complex.new(-1, 1):conj() -- results in -1-1i
```

luaL_Reg
> A C struct that represents a named C function:

```
typedef struct luaL_Reg {
  const char *name;
  lua_CFunction func;
} luaL_Reg;
```

void luaL_newlib(lua_State *L,
                 const luaL_Reg list[]);   **Lua 5.2, 5.3, 5.4**
> Pushes onto the stack a new table composed of the C functions in NULL-terminated list *list*.

int luaL_newmetatable(lua_State *L, const char *name);
> Pushes onto the stack the metatable identified by string *name*, and returns 1 if the metatable had to be created first or 0 if the metatable already existed.

CAUTION

Lua keeps track of all metatable names in the same place. If the host loads any external C modules, those modules will also have the ability to create their own metatables, so there is a possibility of name clashes.

---

void luaL_setfuncs(lua_State *L, const luaL_Reg *list,
                   int n);   **Lua 5.2, 5.3, 5.4**
> Pops *n* values off the stack, associates them with the C functions in NULL-terminated list *list* as upvalues, and adds the resulting closures to the table that is now at the top of the stack, that was originally below the *n* values.

void luaL_requiref(lua_State *L, const char *name,
                   lua_CFunction f,
                   int global);   **Lua 5.2, 5.3, 5.4**
> Mimics Lua's require() function by calling function *f* with string *name* as an argument and registering the value returned by *f* as the module named *name*. If *global* is nonzero, assigns the returned value to the global variable whose name is *name*. Only the first value returned by *f* is used and left on the stack.

> Subsequent calls to luaL_requiref() with *name* will produce the original value returned by *f*.

```
void luaL_register(lua_State *L, const char *name,
                   const luaL_Reg *list);                    Lua 5.1
```
Pushes onto the stack a new table composed of the C functions in NULL-terminated list *list*, registers that table as the module named *name*, and assigns it to the global variable whose name is *name*. If *name* is NULL, adds all functions in *list* to the table at the top of the stack.

Error and Warning Handling

Properly handling Lua errors in C is vitally important. Whenever Lua raises an error (either on its own or from an explicit API call), it uses C's function longjmp() in an attempt to handle the error. Unless the error occurred within a protected call, Lua's panic function is invoked, and a hard abort will occur unless the host intervenes and performs a longjmp() of its own to recover. By contrast, a protected call catches and handles the error gracefully, and returns an error code. The API functions lua_pcall(), lua_cpcall(), luaL_dofile(), luaL_dostring(), lua_resume(), and lua_pcallk() are all protected calls. The first two are described in the section "Call a C Function" on page 121, the next two are described in the section "Load and Run Dynamic Code" on page 131, and the last two are covered in the section "Threading in C" on page 133. Each of those sections has an example that demonstrates how to handle errors with their respective API functions. Table 15 lists the error codes that protected calls can return, along with their meanings.

Table 15. Error codes returned by protected calls

Error code	Meaning
LUA_OK[a]	Success
LUA_ERRRUN	Runtime error
LUA_ERRMEM	Memory allocation error
LUA_ERRERR	Error running the error handler given to lua_pcall() or lua_pcallk()

[a] Not in Lua 5.1, which uses the constant 0 instead.

Sometimes Lua cannot raise an error in a defined context, such as while closing a to-be-closed variable, and during garbage collection. In cases like these, Lua 5.4 emits a warning, which can either be handled or ignored. (Lua 5.1, 5.2 and 5.3, however, will simply raise the error in an arbitrary context.) Lua's default behavior is to print warnings to standard error (stderr).

```
lua_CFunction lua_atpanic(lua_State *L, lua_CFunction f);
```
Designates C function *f* as the function Lua calls when an unexpected error occurs, and returns the previously designated panic function. When *f* is called, the error message is at the top of the stack.

After the panic function returns, Lua aborts the host application. This unhappy outcome can be avoided if the host performs a `longjmp()` of its own to recover.

```
lua_setwarnf(lua_State *L, lua_WarnFunction f,
           void *data);                              Lua 5.4
```
Designates C function *f* as the function Lua calls to emit warnings. *f* has the following type:

```
typedef void (*lua_WarnFunction) (void *data,
                                  const char *message,
                                  int tocontinue);
```

f is called with *data*, a string warning message, and a flag that indicates whether or not the next call's message is a continuation of the previous call's message.

WARNING

f should not utilize *L* while handling a warning.

Retrieve Error Information

In addition to having the error message at the top of the stack after an error occurred, the host can also retrieve a traceback with additional error information.

```
void luaL_traceback(lua_State *L, lua_State *L1,
                    const char *message,
                    int level);                   Lua 5.2, 5.3, 5.4
```
Pushes onto the stack a string traceback of the call stack

in thread *L1* at call level number *level*, with optional string message *message* prepended to the traceback. A *level* of 0 is the current function (or the current file or module if there is no current function), 1 is the function that called the current function, 2 is the caller of the function that called the current function, and so on.

Load and Run Dynamic Code

The host can load and execute user-provided chunks of Lua code at run-time. It can also do this in a sandboxed environment as a security measure. Example 32 illustrates how the host can run user-defined Lua scripts in a tightly-controlled environment that does not provide access to external modules, the underlying filesystem and operating system, and any other potentially unsafe Lua features.

Example 32. Run user-defined Lua code in a sandbox

```
// Define and store the sandbox for subsequent use.
const char *safe[] = {
  "assert", "error", "ipairs", "math", "next", "pairs",
  "pcall", "select", "string", "table", "tonumber",
  "tostring", "type", "xpcall", NULL
};
lua_newtable(L); // the sandbox environment
for (const char **p = safe; *p; p++)
  lua_getglobal(L, *p), lua_setfield(L, -2, *p);
/* add other safe host functions to sandbox... */
int sandbox_ref = luaL_ref(L, LUA_REGISTRYINDEX);

/* ... */

// Attempt to load the user-defined Lua script
// (text-only) as an anonymous function.
if (luaL_loadfilex(L, user_script, "t") == LUA_OK) {
  // Make the sandbox the function's environment.
  lua_rawgeti(L, LUA_REGISTRYINDEX, sandbox_ref);
  lua_setupvalue(L, -2, 1);
  // Execute the script.
  if (lua_pcall(L, 0, 0, 0) != LUA_OK) {
    /* process and pop error message at index -1... */
  }
}
```

```
/* ... */

// Finished with the sandbox; delete it.
luaL_unref(L, LUA_REGISTRYINDEX, sandbox_ref);
```

```
int luaL_dostring(lua_State *L, const char *s);
int luaL_dofile  (lua_State *L, const char *filename);
```

Executes the contents of string *s* or the file identified by
string *filename* as a chunk of Lua code, pushes onto the
stack all values returned by that chunk, and returns
LUA_OK (or 0 in Lua 5.1) on success.

If an error occurred, a non-zero error code is returned
and the error message is pushed onto the stack instead.
In addition to the error codes listed in Table 15 on page
129, LUA_ERRSYNTAX and LUA_ERRFILE can also be returned,
which indicate there was a syntax error or problem
opening the file, respectively.

```
int luaL_loadstring (lua_State *L, const char *s);
int luaL_loadbuffer (lua_State *L, const char *s,
                     size_t len, const char *name);
int luaL_loadbufferx(lua_State *L, const char *s,
                     size_t len, const char *name,
                     const char *mode);      Lua 5.2, 5.3, 5.4
int luaL_loadfile   (lua_State *L, const char *filename);
int luaL_loadfilex  (lua_State *L, const char *filename,
                     const char *mode);      Lua 5.2, 5.3, 5.4
```

Loads as a chunk of Lua code zero-terminated string *s*,
string *s* of length *len* bytes, or the contents of the file
identified by string *filename*, pushes onto the stack a Lua
function that will execute that chunk when called, and
returns LUA_OK (or 0 in Lua 5.1) on success. *name* is an optional string name associated with the chunk and *mode* indicates whether the chunk can be text ("t"), binary
("b"), or both ("bt"). The default value of *mode* is "bt".
(Binary chunks are produced by Lua's *luac* or *lu
ac.exe* executable.)

If an error occurred, a non-zero error code is returned
and the error message is pushed onto the stack instead.
In addition to the error codes listed in Table 15 on page
129, LUA_ERRSYNTAX and LUA_ERRFILE can also be returned.
The former indicates there was a syntax error and the
latter indicates there was a problem opening the file.

CAUTION

Lua does not verify the integrity of, or in any way sanitize binary chunks. Running truly arbitrary binary chunks may be unsafe.

```
const char *lua_setupvalue(lua_State *L,
                           int index, 1);        Lua 5.2, 5.3, 5.4
int         lua_setfenv (lua_State *L, int index);   Lua 5.1
```
Pops a table value off the stack, designates it as the environment of the function value at stack index *index*, and returns non-NULL or 1 on success. The section "Environments" on page 46 describes environments.

Threading in C

The host can create and use threads similarly to how Lua can create and use threads as illustrated in the section "Thread Facilities" on page 68. However, the typical threading procedure in C differs slightly from the threading procedure in Lua:

1. The main Lua thread creates and pushes a new (suspended) thread *T* onto the stack.

2. The main thread pushes a function body onto the stack of *T*. (*T* has its own stack, but shares the same global environment.)

3. Upon starting *T*, the main thread is temporarily suspended, and the body of *T* is executed.

4. *T* performs some work and then yields back to the main thread.

5. The main thread resumes right where it left off, at the point where it started *T*. *T* is now suspended.

6. The main thread performs some work and then resumes *T*.

7. *T* resumes, but not right where it left off (at the point where it yielded back to the main thread). Instead, *T* either resumes in the caller of the function that yielded *T*, or resumes in the *continuation function* specified by the function that yielded *T*. The main thread is now suspended.

8. This process repeats until *T* completes its work and the

thread finishes.

9. The main thread resumes right where it left off and continues indefinitely. *T* is now dead and cannot be resumed.

During each transition between threads, values can be exchanged between the thread stacks. When the main thread starts *T*, it can pass values from its stack to the function body of *T*. When *T* yields, it can pass values from its stack back to the main thread's stack. When the main thread resumes *T*, it can pass more of its stack values to *T*. And so on.

Example 33 illustrates the entirety of this typical threading procedure by starting a series of threads that continuously monitor files for output, by having those threads pass that output back to the main thread for processing, and by having the main thread ask monitoring threads to stop monitoring based on their processed output. (While this example operates on files, it can be adapted to work on other resources like sockets and pipes.)

In addition to the typical threading procedure, there is a quirk involving a C function that calls another function that eventually yields. This case is also handled using continuation functions.

All of the aforementioned aspects of threading in C, including continuation functions, are described in the following sections.

Example 33. Monitor output from a set of files

```
// Filenames to monitor.
const char *filenames[32]; // should have NULL sentinel

/* ... */

// Thread body continuation function for monitoring a
// file.
static int monitor(lua_State *thread, int status,
                   lua_KContext ctx) {
  FILE *f = (FILE*)ctx;
  // Stop monitoring file if requested to.
  if (status == LUA_YIELD &&
      !lua_toboolean(thread, 1)) {
    fclose(f);
```

```
    return 0;
  }
  // Check for data to be read.
  int c = getc(f);
  if (c != EOF) {
    // Read and yield a line of data.
    ungetc(c, f);
    char buf[BUFSIZ];
    fgets(buf, BUFSIZ, f);
    lua_pushstring(thread, buf);
    return lua_yieldk(thread, 1, ctx, monitor);
  } else {
    // No data to read; yield nothing.
    return lua_yieldk(thread, 0, ctx, monitor);
  }
}

// Thread body function for monitoring a file.
static int monitor_file(lua_State *thread) {
  const char *filename = luaL_checkstring(thread, 1);
  FILE *f = fopen(filename, "r");
  if (!f)
    return luaL_error(thread, "file '%s' not found",
                      filename);
  lua_settop(thread, 0); // clear
  return monitor(thread, LUA_OK, (lua_KContext)f);
}

/* ... */

// Create and start threads.
lua_createtable(L, 32, 0); // active threads table
for (int i = 0; i < 32; i++) {
  if (!filenames[i]) break;
  lua_State *thread = lua_newthread(L);
  lua_pushcfunction(thread, monitor_file);
  lua_pushstring(thread, filenames[i]);
  int nresults; // unused
  if (lua_resume(thread, L, 1, &nresults) == LUA_YIELD)
    // Store thread for monitoring.
    lua_rawseti(L, -2, lua_rawlen(L, -2) + 1);
  else {
    /* handle error starting thread... */
    lua_pop(L, 1);
  }
}
```

```
// Monitor active threads.
int i = 1;
while (lua_rawlen(L, -1) > 0) {
  lua_rawgeti(L, -1, i);
  lua_State *thread = lua_tothread(L, -1);
  if (lua_gettop(thread) > 0) {
    // Thread has output from its monitored file.
    const char *line = lua_tostring(thread, -1);
    /* process line and possibly stop monitoring... */
    lua_pushboolean(thread, keep_monitoring);
    lua_replace(thread, 1);
    int nresults; // unused
    lua_resume(thread, L, 1, &nresults);
    if (!keep_monitoring) {
      // Stop monitoring the now-dead thread.
      lua_getglobal(L, "table");
      lua_getfield(L, -1, "remove");
      lua_replace(L, -2);
      lua_pushvalue(L, -3); // active threads table
      lua_pushnumber(L, i);
      lua_call(L, 2, 0); // table.remove(threads, i)
      lua_pop(L, 1); // dead thread
      continue; // monitor next thread
    }
  }
  lua_pop(L, 1); // thread
  if (++i > lua_rawlen(L, -1)) i = 1; // start again
}
lua_pop(L, 1); // active threads table
```

Create a Thread

The host can create threads. Each thread has its own stack for
pushing values onto (such as a function body) and popping
values off of (such as return values).

lua_State
> A C **struct** that represents both a thread in a Lua inter-
> preter and the interpreter itself.

lua_State *lua_newthread(lua_State *L);
> Creates and pushes onto the stack a new (suspended)
> thread and returns a pointer to it. The new thread has its
> own stack, but shares the same global environment as
> Lua interpreter L.

Start or Resume a Thread

The host can start a thread that has a function body on its stack and can resume a thread that had previously yielded.

void lua_pushcfunction(lua_State *thread, lua_CFunction f);
 Pushes C function value f onto the stack of thread thread.

int lua_resume(lua_State *thread, lua_State *L, int nargs,
          int *nresults); **Lua 5.4**
int lua_resume(lua_State *thread, lua_State *L,
          int nargs); **Lua 5.2, 5.3**
int lua_resume(lua_State *thread, int nargs); **Lua 5.1**
 Starts or resumes execution of thread thread from thread L (the currently active thread), and returns LUA_OK (or 0 in Lua 5.1) if thread finishes without error, LUA_YIELD if thread subsequently yields, or a non-zero error code if thread raises an error. Table 15 on page 129 lists Lua's error codes and their meanings.

 When starting thread, nargs function argument values are popped off the stack of thread, the thread function body now at the top of the stack is popped off the stack, and that popped function is called with the popped arguments (the last value popped being the first argument and the first value popped being the last argument).

 When resuming thread, all values on its stack are either left for the continuation function passed to the call to lua_yieldk() that originally yielded thread, left for the caller of lua_yield(), or used as the return values of the yielding call to coroutine.yield().

 If thread subsequently yields without error, the top nre sults on its stack (which happen to be the only values on the stack in Lua 5.1, 5.2, and 5.3) are the argument values specified by the yielding call. If thread finishes without error, the top nresults values on its stack (the only stack values in Lua 5.1, 5.2, and 5.3) are the values returned by the function body of thread. If thread raises an error, the error message is at the top of its stack.

Yield a Thread

The host can yield the running thread. After a C function yields, it is impossible to return to that function when the thread resumes, due to the nature of the yield. Instead, Lua 5.2, 5.3, and 5.4 allow for a continuation function to be called upon resumption. Lua 5.1 simply returns to the caller of the C function.

int lua_isyieldable(lua_State *L, int *index*);   **Lua 5.3, 5.4**
> Returns 1 if the value at stack index *index* is a yieldable thread. Otherwise, returns 0.

lua_KFunction   **Lua 5.3, 5.4**
> The C type associated with continuation functions:
>
> ```
> typedef int (*lua_KFunction) (lua_State *thread,
>                               int status,
>                               lua_KContext ctx);
> ```
>
> When a continuation function is called by Lua, status is LUA_YIELD. When calling a continuation function manually, status is either LUA_OK, or the non-zero error code returned by lua_pcallk() if an error occurred.

lua_KContext   **Lua 5.3, 5.4**
> The C type associated with continuation function contexts (typically intptr_t or ptrdiff_t, which are large enough to store an arbitrary pointer). Continuation function contexts are unused by Lua, but may be useful to the host for passing around state information.

int lua_getctx(lua_State *thread*, int *ctx*);   **Lua 5.2**
> Returns LUA_YIELD if the current function was called by Lua to continue from a yield, and sets *ctx* to the value passed to the call to lua_yieldk() that yielded thread *thread*. Otherwise, returns LUA_OK and leaves *ctx* unmodified.

int lua_yieldk(lua_State *thread*, int *nresults*,
               lua_KContext *ctx*, lua_KFunction *k*); **Lua 5.3, 5.4**
int lua_yieldk(lua_State *thread*, int *nresults*,
            int *ctx*, lua_CFunction *k*);   **Lua 5.2**
int lua_yield (lua_State *thread*, int *nresults*);
> Yields thread *thread*, and either leaves only the top *nresults* values on its stack for use by the lua_resume() call

that originally started or resumed *thread*, or uses those values as the (potentially extra) return values of the Lua call that originally started or resumed *thread*.

When *thread* is resumed again, *k*(*thread*, LUA_YIELD, *ctx*) is called (or just *k*(*thread*) in Lua 5.2), and the only values on the stack of *thread* are either the values left by the resuming lua_resume() call, or the argument values passed to the resuming Lua call. If there is no continuation function (which is always the case in Lua 5.1), execution returns to the original caller of this function.

Transfer Values Between Threads

When a thread yields, the host can transfer that thread's stack values to the main thread (or any other live thread). Similarly, the host can transfer values from the stack of another live thread to the thread about to be resumed.

void lua_xmove(lua_State *from*, lua_State *to*, int *n*);
Pops *n* values off the stack of thread *from* and pushes them onto the stack of thread *to*. Both *from* and *to* must share the same Lua interpreter.

Query a Thread's Status

The host can query the status of a thread.

int lua_status(lua_State *thread*);
Returns the status of thread *thread*: LUA_OK (or 0 in Lua 5.1) for a normal thread (active but not running, not yet started, or finished without error), LUA_YIELD if *thread* has yielded, or the non-zero error code returned by lua_re sume() if *thread* raised an error. Table 15 on page 129 lists Lua's error codes and their meanings.

Close a Thread

The host can close a thread in Lua 5.4, though this is typically only done when that thread has variables that need to be closed and either it is suspended and not expected to be resumed, or an error has occurred inside of it.

```
int lua_resetthread(lua_State *thread);                    Lua 5.4
```
Closes thread *thread* and its to-be-closed variables, and returns LUA_OK if no error occurred during the closing process. Otherwise, returns a non-zero error code and pushes the error message onto the stack.

Call a Function that Yields

Any running thread (including the main thread) can invoke functions, including C functions. These C functions can in turn invoke other functions. A potential problem may arise if a C function *f* invokes another function that ultimately yields. When the suspended thread resumes, it is impossible to return to *f* due to the nature of the yield. While Lua 5.1 will throw an error at this attempt to "yield across a C-call boundary," Lua 5.2, 5.3, and 5.4 allow for a continuation function to be called upon resumption. Example 34 demonstrates how to handle this case as it iterates over all key-value pairs in a table and calls a potentially yielding function with each pair as arguments.

Example 34. Call a function for each table key-value pair

```
// Thread body continuation function for iterating over
// a table's key-value pairs and calling a function
// with each pair as that function's arguments.
static int iterator(lua_State *thread, int status,
                    lua_KContext ctx) {
  if (status == LUA_OK)
    lua_pushnil(thread); // start iteration
  else
    lua_pop(thread, 1); // previous value
  while (lua_next(thread, 1) != 0) {
    lua_pushvalue(thread, lua_upvalueindex(1));
    lua_pushvalue(thread, -3); // key
    lua_pushvalue(thread, -3); // value
    lua_callk(thread, 2, 0, 0, iterator);
    lua_pop(thread, 1); // value
  }
  return 0;
}

// Initial thread body function.
static int iterate(lua_State *thread) {
  return iterator(thread, LUA_OK, 0);
```

```
}
/* ... */

lua_State *thread = lua_newthread(L);
/* push function to be called each iteration... */
lua_pushcclosure(thread, iterate, 1);
/* push table to be iterated over... */
int nresults;
while (lua_resume(thread, L, 1, &nresults) ==
        LUA_YIELD) {
  /* work to do in-between yields... */
  lua_pop(thread, nresults);
}
lua_pop(L, 1); // dead thread
```

lua_KFunction   **Lua 5.3, 5.4**
The C type associated with continuation functions:

```
typedef int (*lua_KFunction) (lua_State *thread,
                              int status,
                              lua_KContext ctx);
```

When a continuation function is called by Lua, status is
LUA_YIELD. When calling a continuation function manually, status is either LUA_OK, or the non-zero error code
returned by lua_pcallk() if an error occurred.

lua_KContext   **Lua 5.3, 5.4**
The C type associated with continuation function contexts (typically intptr_t or ptrdiff_t, which are large
enough to store an arbitrary pointer). Continuation function contexts are unused by Lua, but may be useful to
the host for passing around state information.

int lua_getctx(lua_State *thread, int *ctx);   **Lua 5.2**
Returns LUA_YIELD if the current function was called by
Lua to continue from a yield, and sets ctx to the value
passed to the call to lua_yieldk() that yielded thread
thread. If the current function was called by Lua after an
error occurred in a call to lua_pcallk(), returns a non-
zero error code and sets ctx to the value passed to
lua_pcallk(). Otherwise, returns LUA_OK and leaves ctx
unmodified. Table 15 on page 129 lists Lua's error codes
and their meanings.

```
void lua_callk(lua_State *thread, int nargs, int nresults,
               lua_KContext ctx, lua_KFunction k);  Lua 5.3, 5.4
void lua_callk(lua_State *thread, int nargs, int nresults,
               int ctx, lua_CFunction k);                    Lua 5.2
int lua_pcallk(lua_State *thread, int nargs, int nresults,
               int error_handler, lua_KContext ctx,
               lua_KFunction k);                        Lua 5.3, 5.4
int lua_pcallk(lua_State *thread, int nargs, int nresults,
               int error_handler, int ctx,
               lua_CFunction k);                             Lua 5.2
```

Pops *nargs* function argument values off the stack, pops off the stack the function that is now at the top of the stack, calls that popped function with the popped arguments (the last value popped being the first argument and the first value popped being the last argument), and pushes the first *nresults* values returned by the function onto the stack (or all of them if *nresults* is LUA_MULTRET). lua_pcallk() returns LUA_OK on success.

lua_callk() should only be called from within C functions that do not care to handle errors and have been ultimately invoked by a protected call. The section "Error and Warning Handling" on page 129 describes protected calls.

If an error occurs, lua_pcallk() pushes the error message onto the stack and returns a non-zero error code. If *error_handler* is nonzero, the function at stack index *error_handler* is called with the error message as an argument, and that function's return value is the error message ultimately pushed onto the stack. Table 15 on page 129 lists Lua's error codes and their meanings.

If *thread* yields during the call, the original lua_callk() or lua_pcallk() call will not return. Instead, whenever *thread* resumes, k(*thread*, LUA_YIELD, *ctx*) is called (or just k(*thread*) in Lua 5.2), and the stack contains the first *nresults* values returned by the originally called function (or all of the returned values if *nresults* is LUA_MULTRET).

If the value being called is a table or userdata value with the metamethod __call(), that metamethod is called to perform the operation. The section "Other Operator and Statement Metamethods" on page 35 covers this metamethod in its generic form.

Memory Management

Lua manages the memory of its values by allocating memory for new values and freeing memory for values no longer in use. Lua employs a garbage collector to automatically detect and delete unused values. More often than not this is sufficient. However, Lua provides access controls for its collector should the need arise.

```
int lua_gc(lua_State *L, LUA_GCCOLLECT, 0);
```
Performs a full garbage collection cycle.

```
int lua_gc(lua_State *L, LUA_GCSTOP, 0);
int lua_gc(lua_State *L, LUA_GCRESTART, 0);
```
Stops and restarts automatic garbage collection.

```
int lua_gc(lua_State *L, LUA_GCISRUNNING, 0);
```
Returns 1 if automatic garbage collection is on and 0 if it is off.

```
int lua_gc(lua_State *L, LUA_GCCOUNT, 0);
```
Returns the number of kilobytes of memory used by Lua.

Miscellaneous

Lua provides other miscellaneous C API facilities.

```
int lua_numbertointeger(lua_Number n,
                        lua_Integer *i);          Lua 5.3, 5.4
```
Converts float *n* to an integer, stores the result in *i*, and returns 1 or, if the conversion fails, returns 0.

```
size_t lua_stringtonumber(lua_State *L,
                          const char *s);          Lua 5.3, 5.4
```
Converts string *s* to a number and, if successful, pushes that number onto the stack and returns a number greater than zero. A return value of 0 indicates the conversion failed and that nothing was pushed.

```
void lua_pushglobaltable(lua_State *L);    Lua 5.2, 5.3, 5.4
lua_pushvalue(L, LUA_GLOBALSINDEX);                Lua 5.1
```
Pushes the global environment table onto the stack.

int lua_setiuservalue(lua_State *L, int *index*,
                        int *n*);   **Lua 5.4**
void lua_setuservalue (lua_State *L,
                        int *index*);   **Lua 5.2, 5.3, 5.4**
int lua_setfenv   (lua_State *L, int *index*);   **Lua 5.1**
Pops a value off the stack (which must be a table in Lua
5.1, or a table or nil in Lua 5.2), associates it as the nth
(or only) user value of the full userdata value at stack index *index*, and returns 1 if the operation succeeded. Otherwise, returns 0.

int lua_getiuservalue(lua_State *L, int *index*,
                        int *n*);   **Lua 5.4**
int lua_getuservalue (lua_State *L, int *index*);   **Lua 5.3, 5.4**
void lua_getuservalue (lua_State *L, int *index*);   **Lua 5.2**
void lua_getfenv   (lua_State *L, int *index*);   **Lua 5.1**
Pushes onto the stack the nth (or only) user value associated with the full userdata value at stack index *index*,
and returns the pushed value's type. In Lua 5.1 the
pushed value is always a table, and in Lua 5.2 it is always either a table or nil.

void lua_getfenv(lua_State *L, int *index*);   **Lua 5.1**
Pushes onto the stack the environment table of the function or thread value at stack index *index*.

Lua and C API Index

---

luaL_* (continued)
luaL_optint, 118
luaL_optinteger, 118
luaL_optlong, 118
luaL_optlstring, 118
luaL_optnumber, 118
luaL_optstring, 118
luaL_optunsigned, 118
luaL_prepbuffer, 96
luaL_prepbuffsize, 96
luaL_pushresult, 96
luaL_pushresultsize, 96
luaL_ref, 114

luaL_Reg, 128
luaL_register, 129
luaL_requiref, 89, 128
luaL_setfuncs, 128
luaL_setmetatable, 123
luaL_testudata, 117
luaL_tolstring, 104
luaL_traceback, 130
luaL_typeerror, 117
luaL_typename, 102
luaL_typerror, 117
luaL_unref, 114

Concept Index

Lua interpreter,
  closing, 89
  creating, 89
  stand-alone, 1, 5, 87
LuaJIT, 1

M

main thread, 89
mathematical functions, 51
memory management, 82,
  143
metamethods, 32-38
  arithmetic, 33
  bitwise, 34
  bypassing, 38
  concatenation, 36
  function, 37
  function call, 36
  garbage collection, 99
  invoking in C, 124
  length, 37
  relational, 33
  table index, 36
  table iteration, 37
metatables, 32, 122-124
  assigning, 32, 123
  creating in C, 123
  retrieving, 32, 123
modules, 42-46, 124-129
  creating, 45, 124, 128
  loading, 5, 43, 89, 128
  unloading, 44
multi-line comments, 9
multi-line strings, 13
multi-threading (see threads)

N

nil, 12
  pushing (stack), 92
numbers, 12
  pushing (stack), 92
  retrieving (stack), 103
numeric for loop, 25

O

object-oriented
  programming, 38-42
  classes, defining, 38-41
  classes, invoking, 41
  inheritance, 40
  methods, defining, 41
  multiple inheritance, 41
opening files (see files)
operator overloading, 32
operators, 17-23
  arithmetic, 17
  bitwise, 20
  concatenation, 22
  function call, 21
  length, 22
  logical, 19
  overloading, 32
  precedence of, 17
  relational, 18
  table index, 22
  ternary, 20

P

Parsing Expression
  Grammars, 42
patterns, 60-62
prime number
  generation, 25
processes, 78
protected calls, 48, 129

R

random numbers, 53
read-only tables, 36
reading from files (see files)
reference system, 113
registry, 113
regular expressions, 60
relational operators, 18
  invoking (stack), 107
  metamethods for, 33
repeat until loop, 26

retrieving (stack), 104
starting, 70, 137
transferring data between
    in C, 139
yielding, 70, 138
times and dates, 79-81
to-be-closed variables, 11,
    35
    metamethod for, 35
trigonometric functions, 52
types, 12-16
    boolean, 12
    converting between, 16,
        143
    determining, 16, 101
    function, 14
    nil, 12
    number, 12
    string, 13
    table, 15
    thread, 15
    userdata, 16

U
unit testing, 42
upvalues, 4, 28, 96, 119

URL parser, 60
user values, 98
userdata, 16, 98-100
    full userdata, 98
    light userdata, 98
    pushing (stack), 98-100
    retrieving (stack), 105
UTF-8 strings, 63

V
values (see types)
variables,
    assigning, 23
    attributes for, 11, 100
    global, 10, 46, 106
    local, 10
    multiple assignment, 23
    scope of, 10
    swapping values of, 24
    to-be-closed, 11, 35
vectors, 39

W
warnings, 6, 48, 119, 129
while loop, 26
writing to files (see files)